SCHOLASTIC

Exploring Social Studies 3

Name ______________________________

Class ______________________________

Photo credits and attributions:

p. 16: http://commons.wikimedia.org/wiki/File:Globus.jpg by Stefan Kühn and Fables; p. 31: Fables; p. 43: Fables; p. 44: Fables and http://commons.wikimedia.org/wiki/File:3_types_of_lentil.jpg by Justinc; p. 45: http://commons.wikimedia.org/wiki/File:Ananas~May_2008-1.jpg by Alvesgaspar; http://commons.wikimedia.org/wiki/File:Mango_Alphonso_Ataulfo_Asit.JPG by Asit K. Ghosh; http://commons.wikimedia.org/wiki/File:Broken_Coconut.jpg by Thamizhpparithi Maari; http://commons.wikimedia.org/wiki/File:Jablko.jpg by Pastorius; http://commons.wikimedia.org/wiki/File:Apricot_whole444.jpg by Benjamint444; http://commons.wikimedia.org/wiki/File:Single_strawberry.jpg by Thamizhpparithi Maari; http://commons.wikimedia.org/wiki/File:Ripe_Cherry_(Prunus_avium)_in_Hungary.jpg by Takkk; p. 53: http://commons.wikimedia.org/wiki/File:Saraswati_with_Vitarka_Mudra.JPG by Kristina Kundu; p. 59: http://commons.wikimedia.org/wiki/File:IndianDancer.jpg by Dalbera; http://commons.wikimedia.org/wiki/File:Meenakshi_Payal_bharatanatyam.jpg by Meenakshi Payal; p. 60: http://commons.wikimedia.org/wiki/File:Nandini_Ghosal.jpg by Bala; http://commons.wikimedia.org/wiki/File:Kathakalidancer.jpg by Jovianeye; http://commons.wikimedia.org/wiki/File:Bhangra_Dance_punjab.jpg by Onef9day; http://commons.wikimedia.org/wiki/File:Angami_1863b.jpg by Yves Picq; http://commons.wikimedia.org/wiki/File:Cheraw.jpg by Rmizo; http://commons.wikimedia.org/wiki/File:Jhumur_dance.jpg by rajkuman 1220; http://commons.wikimedia.org/wiki/File:Rakasthani_folk_dance_at_Delhi.jpg by Koshy K; p. 62: http://commons.wikimedia.org/wiki/File:Sarangi_close-up_crop.jpg by Hekerui; http://commons.wikimedia.org/wiki/File:2_dhols.jpg by Nikita Mehta; http://commons.wikimedia.org/wiki/File:Prop._Tabla.jpg by Pakrashi; http://commons.wikimedia.org/wiki/File:Veena.png by Sreejithk2000; http://commons.wikimedia.org/wiki/File:Santoor.jpg by gurmatsangeetorg; p. 65: Fables; p. 66: http://commons.wikimedia.org/wiki/File:Peacock.jpg?uselang=en-gb by Alex Pronove; Fables; p. 73: http://commons.wikimedia.org/wiki/File:India_Gate_-_Delhi,_views_of_India_Gate_(2).JPG by Vinayraj; p. 74: Fables; p. 75: http://commons.wikimedia.org/wiki/File:Jama_Masjid,_Delhi,_main_facade.jpg by Dennis Jarvis; http://commons.wikimedia.org/wiki/File:Qutb_Minar_from_the_Quwwuatul_ul-Islam_mosque,_Qutb_complex.jpg by Fred Hsu; p. 80: http://commons.wikimedia.org/wiki/File:Gateway_of_India.jpg by Rhaessner; http://upload.wikimedia.org/wikipedia/commons/c/c5/Chhatrapati_Shivaji_Terminus_%28Victoria_Terminus%29.jpg by Joe Ravi; p. 85: http://commons.wikimedia.org/wiki/File:Victoria_Memorial,kolkata.jpg by Prantik Mukherjee; p. 86: http://commons.wikimedia.org/wiki/File:St_Paul%27s_Cathedral,_Kolkata.jpg by Jungpionier; p. 90: http://commons.wikimedia.org/wiki/File:Santhome_Basilica.jpg by PlaneMad

First edition 2012
Reprinted 2012, 2013 (twice), 2014 (thrice), 2016, 2017, 2019, 2022, 2025, 2026

ISBN 978-81-8477-937-0

Printed in India at Shiv Shakti Printing and Trading Co., Haryana

Contents

 ISBN 978-81-8477-937-0

Introduction

Exploring Social Studies is an exciting social studies series for levels 1 to 5. The books have been designed to fulfill the requirements of the National Curriculum Framework (NCF), which has been adopted by CBSE, ICSE and major State Educational Boards.

The series adopts a learner-centred approach, encouraging students to make connections between their role in their immediate environment and the world around them. The coursebooks are filled with lots of colourful photographs, maps and illustrations that expose students to real-life everyday experiences from around the world.

In addition, the series prepares students to meet the challenges of the future by

- following pyramidal pedagogy
- encouraging exploration and innovation
- facilitating observation and logical analysis to support conclusions
- promoting independent learning

Learn More provides activities that hone the students' ability to absorb, infer, classify, experiment and predict.

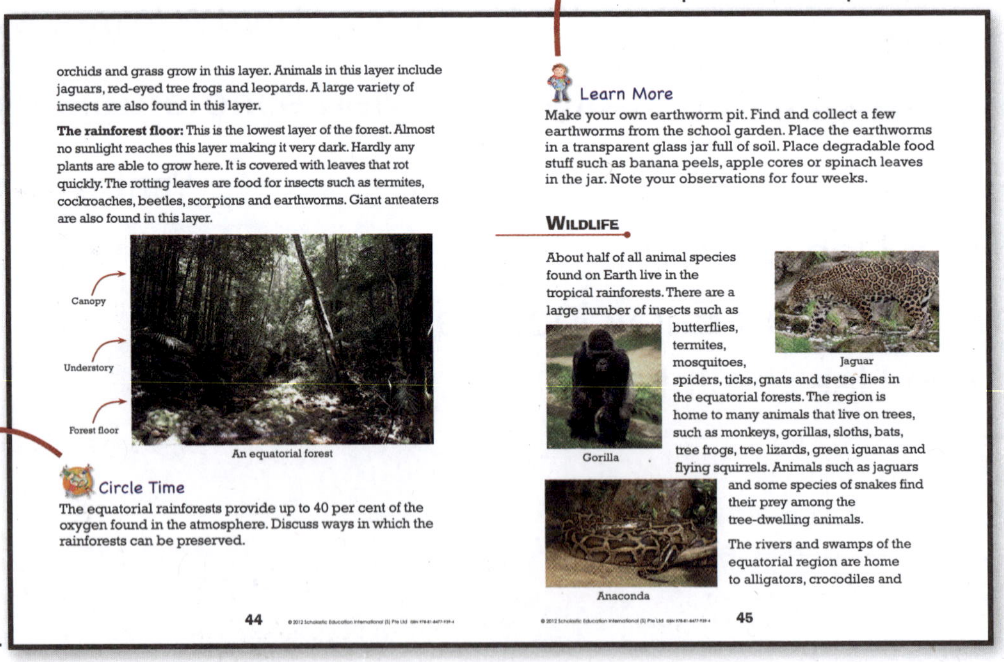
orchids and grass grow in this layer. Animals in this layer include jaguars, red-eyed tree frogs and leopards. A large variety of insects are also found in this layer.

The rainforest floor: This is the lowest layer of the forest. Almost no sunlight reaches this layer making it very dark. Hardly any plants are able to grow here. It is covered with leaves that rot quickly. The rotting leaves are food for insects such as termites, cockroaches, beetles, scorpions and earthworms. Giant anteaters are also found in this layer.

An equatorial forest

Circle Time

The equatorial rainforests provide up to 40 per cent of the oxygen found in the atmosphere. Discuss ways in which the rainforests can be preserved.

44

Learn More

Make your own earthworm pit. Find and collect a few earthworms from the school garden. Place the earthworms in a transparent glass jar full of soil. Place degradable food stuff such as banana peels, apple cores or spinach leaves in the jar. Note your observations for four weeks.

WILDLIFE

About half of all animal species found on Earth live in the tropical rainforests. There are a large number of insects such as butterflies, termites, mosquitoes, spiders, ticks, gnats and tsetse flies in the equatorial forests. The region is home to many animals that live on trees, such as monkeys, gorillas, sloths, bats, tree frogs, tree lizards, green iguanas and flying squirrels. Animals such as jaguars and some species of snakes find their prey among the tree-dwelling animals.

The rivers and swamps of the equatorial region are home to alligators, crocodiles and

Jaguar

Gorilla

Anaconda

45

Circle Time promotes exchange of ideas and techniques while laying emphasis on working as a team.

 ISBN 978-81-8477-937-0

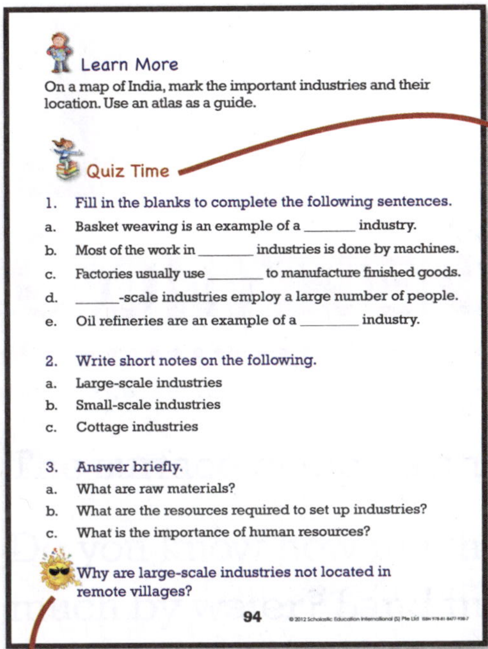

Learn More

On a map of India, mark the important industries and their location. Use an atlas as a guide.

Quiz Time

1. Fill in the blanks to complete the following sentences.
   a. Basket weaving is an example of a _______ industry.
   b. Most of the work in _______ industries is done by machines.
   c. Factories usually use _______ to manufacture finished goods.
   d. _______-scale industries employ a large number of people.
   e. Oil refineries are an example of a _______ industry.
2. Write short notes on the following.
   a. Large-scale industries
   b. Small-scale industries
   c. Cottage industries
3. Answer briefly.
   a. What are raw materials?
   b. What are the resources required to set up industries?
   c. What is the importance of human resources?

Why are large-scale industries not located in remote villages?

94

Factastic imparts interesting information and facts related to the topic under discussion.

Quiz Time tests knowledge retention and serves as a quick recap of the lesson.

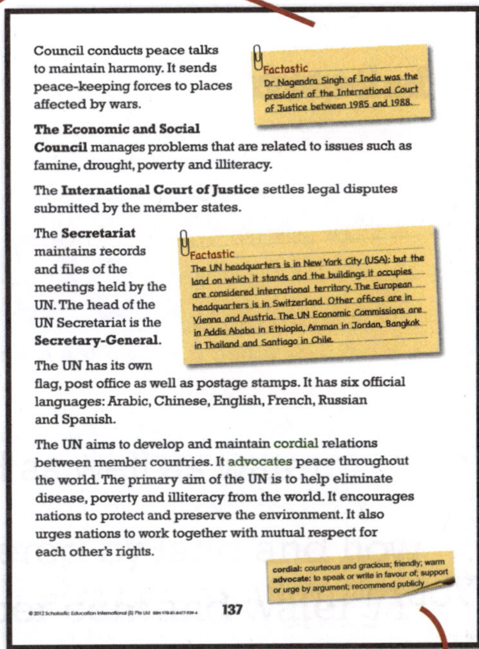

Council conducts peace talks to maintain harmony. It sends peace-keeping forces to places affected by wars.

The Economic and Social Council manages problems that are related to issues such as famine, drought, poverty and illiteracy.

The **International Court of Justice** settles legal disputes submitted by the member states.

The **Secretariat** maintains records and files of the meetings held by the UN. The head of the UN Secretariat is the **Secretary-General.**

Factastic: Dr Nagendra Singh of India was the president of the International Court of Justice between 1985 and 1988.

Factastic: The UN headquarters is in New York City (USA); but the land on which it stands and the buildings it occupies are considered international territory. The European headquarters is in Switzerland. Other offices are in Vienna and Austria. The UN Economic Commissions are in Addis Ababa in Ethiopia, Amman in Jordan, Bangkok in Thailand and Santiago in Chile.

The UN has its own flag, post office as well as postage stamps. It has six official languages: Arabic, Chinese, English, French, Russian and Spanish.

The UN aims to develop and maintain cordial relations between member countries. It advocates peace throughout the world. The primary aim of the UN is to help eliminate disease, poverty and illiteracy from the world. It encourages nations to protect and preserve the environment. It also urges nations to work together with mutual respect for each other's rights.

cordial: courteous and gracious; friendly; warm
advocate: to speak or write in favour of; support or urge by argument; recommend publicly

137

Higher Order Thinking Skills (HOTS) questions are included in levels 4 and 5. These questions sharpen the students' skills of making inferences, understanding the logic behind a concept and thinking outside the box.

New and difficult words are defined in the **glossary**.

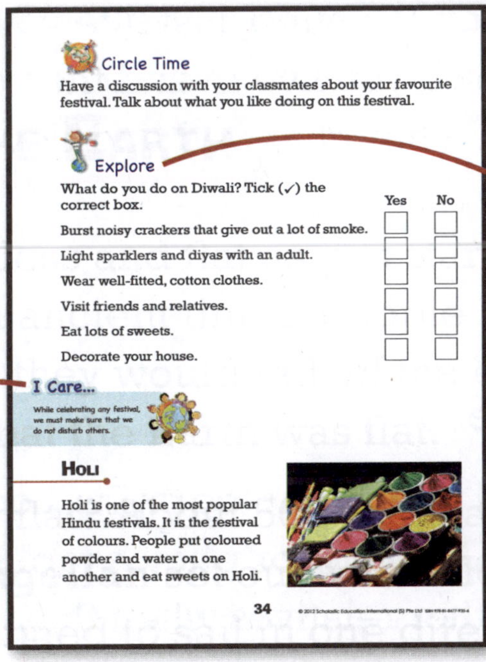

Circle Time

Have a discussion with your classmates about your favourite festival. Talk about what you like doing on this festival.

Explore

What do you do on Diwali? Tick (✓) the correct box.

	Yes	No
Burst noisy crackers that give out a lot of smoke.	☐	☐
Light sparklers and diyas with an adult.	☐	☐
Wear well-fitted, cotton clothes.	☐	☐
Visit friends and relatives.	☐	☐
Eat lots of sweets.	☐	☐
Decorate your house.	☐	☐

I Care... While celebrating any festival, we must make sure that we do not disturb others.

Holi

Holi is one of the most popular Hindu festivals. It is the festival of colours. People put coloured powder and water on one another and eat sweets on Holi.

34

Explore encourages students to analyse and question.

I Care provides value education in levels 1 to 3.

Students are taught to use an atlas, an encyclopedia and the Internet in levels 3 to 5 to do basic research individually and in groups, to present reports and projects. These help build the students' ability to learn independently.

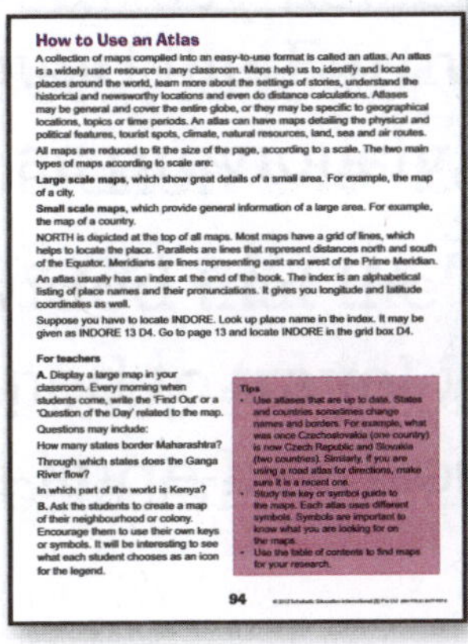

How to Use an Atlas

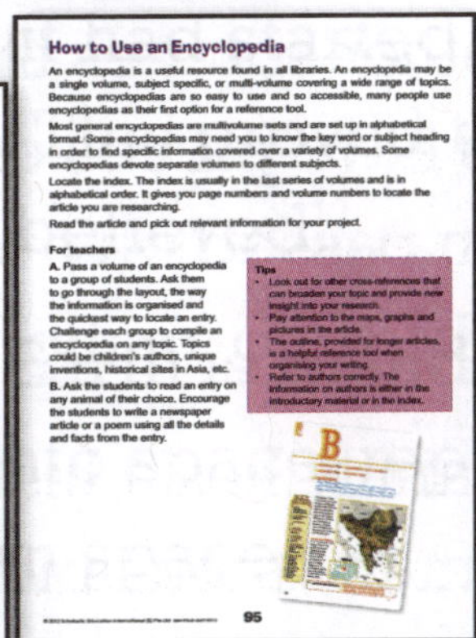

How to Use an Encyclopedia

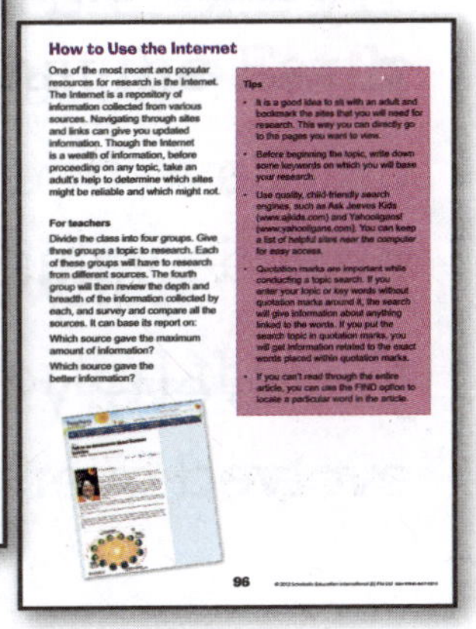

How to Use the Internet

 ISBN 978-81-8477-937-0

1
THE BEGINNING OF TIME

Your family as you see it today was not always the same. Your parents were once children just like you are now. Your grandparents were once young, just like your parents are now. In the same way, the town you live in and the world around you was different in the past. It has changed and developed over time.

Explore

Make a family tree.

Go through your old family photographs. Look for pictures of yourself as a baby. Also look for photographs of your parents, grandparents and other relatives when they were younger.

Try and find other sources that tell you about your family's history. Some families have pieces of jewellery, books or items of clothing that have been passed on from one generation to the next. These provide valuable information about a family's history.

Just as every family has a history, the human family, which has evolved over many thousands of years, also has a history.

 ISBN 978-81-8477-937-0

Historians use information that they gather from studying manuscripts, coins, seals, remains of buildings and palaces, utensils, weapons, paintings, clothes and tools of the past as clues to put together a picture of what happened in the past.

TIMELINES

In order to understand the past, we need to know what happened in the past and when. Hence, it is essential to understand the timelines, or the sequence of events.

In order to understand the events that happened many, many years ago, historians have devised a special system of counting the years. The year of the birth of Jesus Christ is taken to be year zero. We begin our calendar from year 1. So, the first year after Christ was born is written as 1 CE (where CE stands for Christian Era or Common Era). We are currently in 2014 CE, which is 2,014 years after Jesus's birth.

But time existed even before the birth of Christ. So how is that time measured? Historians came up with a plan to count the time before the birth of Christ by counting backwards from the year zero. So, the year just before Christ was born is written as 1 BCE (where BCE stands for Before Christian Era/Before Common Era). When we say that the Great Pyramids were built in 2550 BCE, we mean that they were built 2,550 years before the birth of Christ.

Factastic

The terms CE and BCE came into use very recently. Earlier, the terms used were BC (Before Christ) and AD (Anno Domini).

historians: people who study history
manuscripts: books written by hand
sequence of events: the order in which events appeared or occurred

 ISBN 978-81-8477-937-0

A timeline

Early Humans

The human family evolved many years ago. Early humans were called **hominins**. They used tools for hunting, lived in caves and forests and moved from place to place in small groups in search of food. They covered themselves with leaves or skins of animals. These hominins evolved into early human beings or *Homo sapiens* about 195,000 years ago.

We have been able to find out about these early people from human remains found in Africa, cave paintings, remains of shelters and stone tools.

> **Factastic**
> The scientific name for human beings is **Homo sapiens.**

Evolution of humans

 ISBN 978-81-8477-937-0

Learn More

Use an encyclopedia to find out what the term *Homo sapiens* means.

Tools

Stone Age tools

Gradually, early humans realised that they needed sharp tools to dig out roots and to kill animals for food. They started polishing and sharpening stones, bones and wood to make tools and weapons. They made better tools by striking one stone with another till the stone developed a sharp edge. They hunted small animals and collected wild fruits and plants. They learnt to tie sharp stones to sticks and use them as spears to kill animals. This helped them hunt without getting too close to the animals they were hunting. They also learnt to use these tools for fishing, digging and sewing. As many stone tools were used during this period, it is referred to as the **Stone Age**.

Early humans did not have any language to communicate with so they used hand movements to talk to each other. As humans started to hunt, they started to imitate the calls of different animals.

 ISBN 978-81-8477-937-0

They used these sounds while hunting and when communicating with each other.

Early humans lived in caves to protect themselves from the heat, cold, rain and animals. They moved in groups from place to place in search of food. They hunted animals and gathered fruits and hence are known as **hunter–gatherers**.

Early humans discovered they could keep warm and protect their bodies by wearing the fur and skin of animals. These were their first clothes. They gradually learnt to use stone tools to roughly sew together pieces of fur, skin and leaves to make clothes.

Discovering Fire

Early humans would often see fires breaking out in the forests. They soon realised that fire kept away the cold as well as wild animals. They discovered that they could make fire by rubbing together two stones or sticks. This was a great discovery and it brought about many changes in their lifestyle. They realised that they could keep a fire burning by adding dry leaves and twigs to it. Early humans accidently discovered that fire could be used to cook food, too. They discovered that food tasted better when cooked.

I Care...

Do not play with fire. Always make sure an adult is watching if you must light a fire.

 ISBN 978-81-8477-937-0

Settling Down

As early humans wandered from one place to another, they observed plants growing in the wild. They discovered that whenever they threw away the seeds of the fruits they ate, new plants grew from those seeds. They soon discovered that they could grow their own food and no longer needed to move from place to place in search of food. This is how farming began. As they started to grow their own food, they had to settle down in one place in order to look after the plants. They chose areas near rivers, where the land was suitable for farming. Humans now began to grow more food than they required. They thus had to find ways of storing this extra food.

As early humans started to settle down, they began to live as a community. While some people hunted wild animals, others took up farming. Some made pots that were used for storing surplus grains and, perhaps, water. They began to build houses to live in. This led to the formation of a settlement or a village.

Later, they started to keep animals, such as pigs, goats and sheep, to provide them with meat and milk. Cows were tamed and used in farming.

Transportation

Early humans had to walk long distances and carry heavy loads. As they settled down, they learnt that some animals could be tamed and used for carrying loads and to plough land. Animals made it easier for humans to transport goods.

 ISBN 978-81-8477-937-0

Soon they learnt to tie logs together to make rafts that allowed them to travel and carry heavy loads by river. But travelling and transporting heavy loads by land was still very difficult. They made sledges or carts that could be pulled along the ground. They pushed and pulled heavy loads on sledges. They also used animals to pull the sledges, but this was not easy. The sledges could move only where the ground was smooth.

The Invention of the Wheel

Early humans observed that it was easy to roll down logs from a hill top. They realised that round things could move much more easily. So humans fitted their sledges with pieces of tree trunks such that they could roll. Thus, the wheel was invented.

The invention of the wheel improved the quality of life of early humans. Travel by land became much easier. It was now possible to transport stone boulders to build permanent houses. The invention of the wheel was a turning point for humankind.

Circle Time

Have a class discussion on how life would have been different for humans if the wheel had never been invented.

 ISBN 978-81-8477-937-0

Discovery of Metals

Humans discovered that when some stones were heated, liquids oozed out of them that hardened on cooling. This is how early humans discovered metals such as copper and iron. These metals could be forged to make sharp and sturdy tools for farming and hunting. The metals were also used to make better wheels that improved transportation. The discovery of metals made the tools used by early humans very efficient.

Quiz Time

1. **Fill in the blanks to complete the following sentences.**

a. Early humans were __________ and __________.

b. The earliest human remains have been found in __________.

c. Humans appeared on Earth some __________ years ago.

d. Early humans lived in __________.

e. Early humans tied sharp stones to sticks and used them as __________.

2. **Write about the following in a few sentences.**

a. The discovery of fire

b. Early humans settling in communities

c. Transportation before the invention of the wheel

d. The invention of the wheel

 ISBN 978-81-8477-937-0

3. Use the clues in the brackets to unscramble these words.

a. SRIOTHY (the study of the past) ____________________

b. AANRLECD (used to see the year/dates) ____________________

c. IIEENMTL (the sequence of events) ____________________

d. SEAVC (early humans lived here) ____________________

e. IERF (used by early humans to keep warm and cook)

____

f. EEHWL (its invention was the turning point in human history) ____________________

g. OSTP (used for storing grains) ____________________

h. MARERF (someone who cultivates the land) ____________________

4. Answer the questions.

a. What is a timeline?

b. What do historians use to find out about the past?

c. How do we calculate the years before the birth of Jesus Christ?

d. What kinds of tools were used by early humans? What materials did they use to make these tools?

e. Name three animals you think early humans may have used for carrying loads. Also, name three animals that early humans may have used for farming.

f. What did early humans use fire for? What do modern humans use fire for?

g. Why did early humans settle down?

 ISBN 978-81-8477-937-0

2 MAPS AND DIRECTIONS

A **map** is a drawing of an area. It shows the whole area or a part of it. A map can be big or small and is usually prepared on a flat surface. A book of maps is known as an **atlas**.

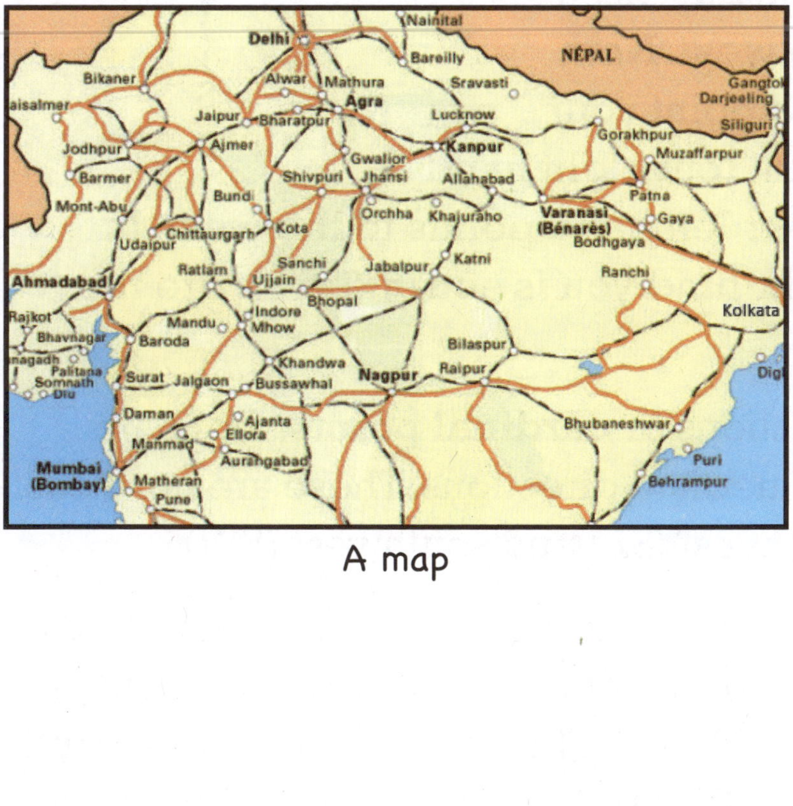

A map

What is a map?

A map is a drawing
To show us the way
To places near our town
And those far away.

The red and black lines
Stand for highways we
take
The blue wiggly lines
Are the rivers and
lakes.

The dots mark the cities
Where most people are
The symbol for
a capital
Is a circle and star.

 ISBN 978-81-8477-937-0

A model of the Earth is known as a **globe**. It shows us the Earth as a whole. We can rotate the globe to see the different places on Earth. The globe provides a very precise depiction of the Earth.

A globe

Learn More

Use an atlas to find the names of the rivers that flow through your state.

DIRECTIONS

Compass rose

Go to an open ground or park in the morning. Stand where you can see the Sun clearly. Remember, the Sun rises in the **east** and sets in the **west**. Now, stretch out your hands and point your right hand towards the Sun. Your right hand now points to the **east**. Your left hand points to the **west**. In front of you is **north** and behind you is **south**. These are the four main directions.

Besides the four main directions or **cardinal points**, there are four subdirections or intermediate directions. These are northeast (NE), northwest (NW), southeast (SE) and southwest (SW).

The top of a map always indicates the north, while the bottom of a map always indicates the south. The direction between north and east is known as the northeast. The direction between south and east is known as the southeast.

 ISBN 978-81-8477-937-0

A compass is a navigational tool for finding directions. It consists of a magnetic pointer that moves freely and aligns itself with the Earth's magnetic poles. It always points to the Earth's magnetic north.

Compass

Factastic

Early sailors studied the position of stars in the night sky and used the compass to navigate the seas. Even now, by studying the stars in the sky, sailors can determine their position and the route they need to take to reach their destination.

Learn More

Fill in the following details about where you live.

a. My house is on a street. The name of the street is ____________.

b. My street is in a neighbourhood. My neighbourhood is called ____________________.

c. My neighbourhood is in a city. The name of my city is ____________________.

d. My city is in a state. My city is in the state of ________________.

e. My state is in a country. The name of my country is ________________________.

I Care...

Do not give out your address or telephone number to strangers. Share these details only with people you know well.

Learn More

Locate your city or town on a map of India.

 ISBN 978-81-8477-937-0

Explore

Use a compass to find out which direction each wall of your classroom faces. Label the classroom walls to indicate which direction they face.

Quiz Time

1. Locate the bank on the map. It is east of Water Street and north of Central Avenue.

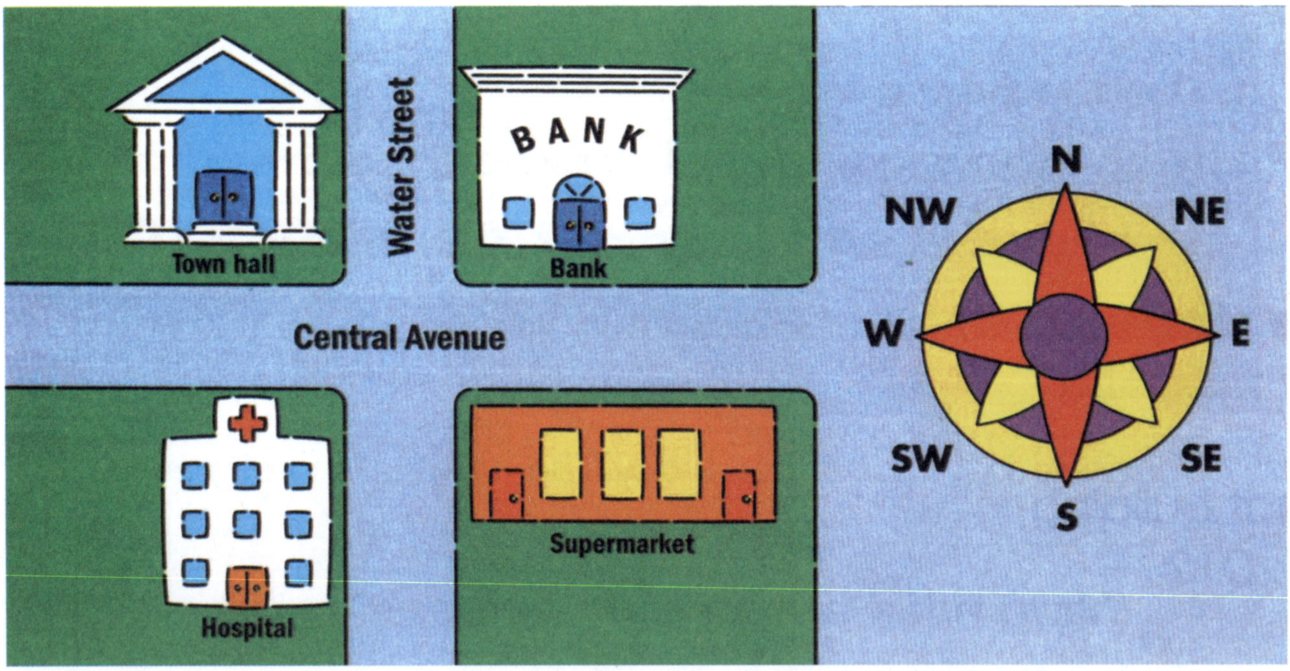

 ISBN 978-81-8477-937-0

Read the map given on the previous page and answer the questions. Colour each compass rose to show the correct direction.

a. In which direction is the Town hall from the hospital?	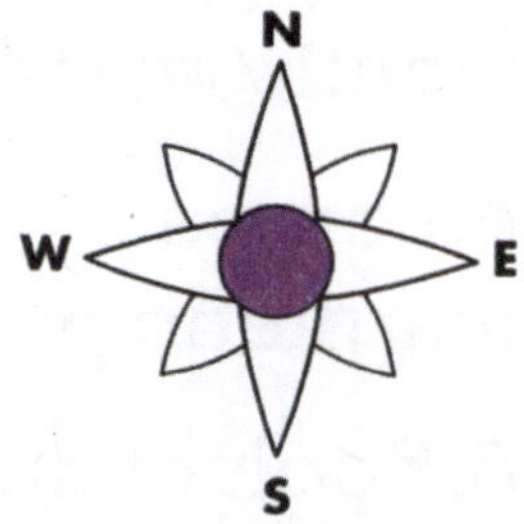
b. On which corner is the supermarket?	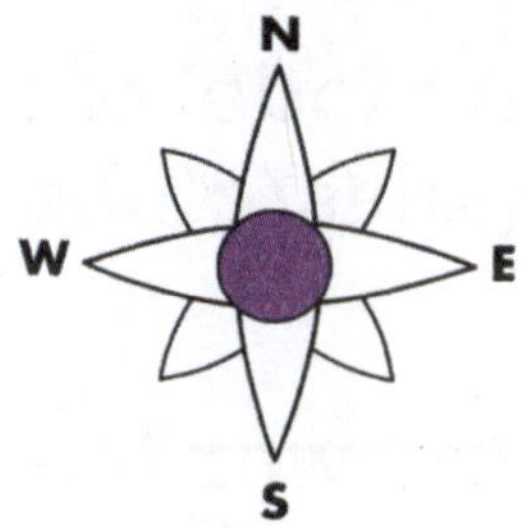
c. On which corner is the hospital?	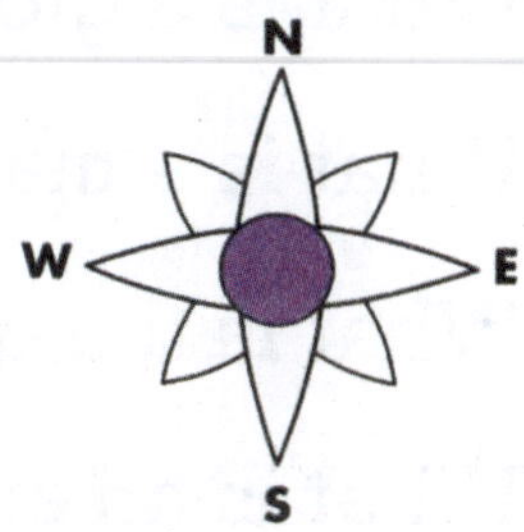
d. You ran out of money at the supermarket. In which direction should you go if you need to get money from the bank?	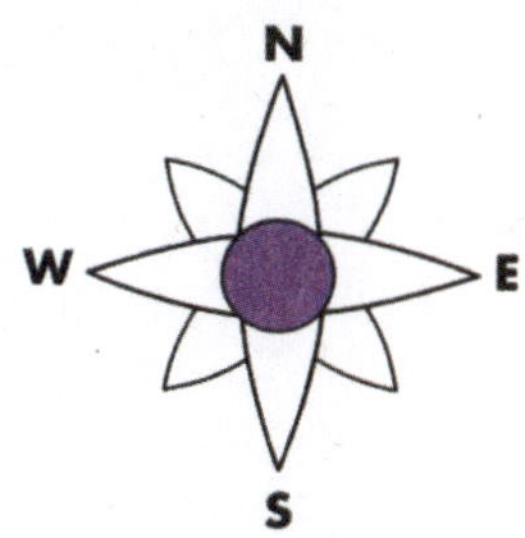
e. In which direction would you go if you wanted to go from the supermarket to the town hall?	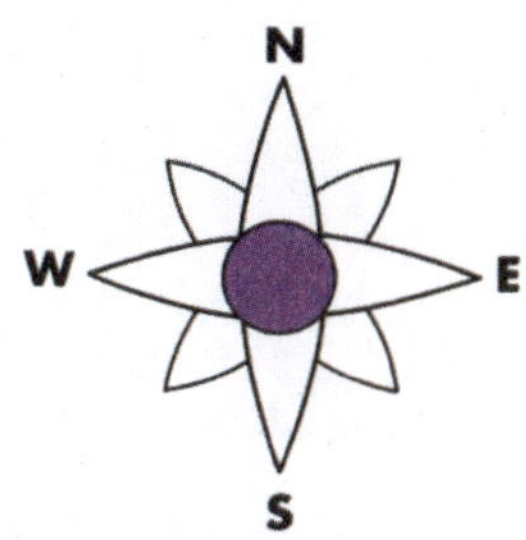

 ISBN 978-81-8477-937-0

2. **Fill in the blanks with the correct words from the brackets.**

a. The blue lines on a map depict ________________. (deserts/rivers/cities)

b. The top of a map always indicates the ________________. (south/west/north)

c. A compass' pointer aligns itself to the ________________ magnetic poles. (globe's/Earth's/atlas')

d. A book of maps is called an ________________. (globe/atlas/compass)

e. A model of the Earth is known as a ________________. (atlas/globe/compass)

3. **Answer the questions.**

a. What is a globe?

b. What is a map? Why do we need it?

c. What is the difference between a globe and a map?

d. What is an atlas?

 ISBN 978-81-8477-937-0

3 Continents and Oceans

The surface of the Earth is covered by land as well as water.

Do you know how much of the Earth is covered by land and how much by water? Land makes up about 29 per cent and water 71 per cent of the Earth's total surface area.

The Shape of the Earth

The Earth seems endless and flat as you stand in an open field or on the seashore. In ancient times, people believed that if they travelled too far, they would fall off the edge of the Earth since they believed that the Earth was flat.

But is the Earth really flat? About 500 years ago, a Portuguese sailor, **Ferdinand Magellan** set out with a fleet of ships from Spain. This fleet continued to sail in one direction and after three years ended up exactly where it had started. The sailors had actually sailed around the Earth. This proved that the Earth was round and not flat as previously believed.

Further proof was provided that the Earth is round when astronauts, people trained to travel into space, reported that the Earth looked like a huge ball from space.

 ISBN 978-81-8477-937-0

The **horizon** is the circular line at which the sky and the Earth appear to meet. If we stand on the shore of the ocean, or on a flat plain, the horizon is a perfect circle, as we will be able to see the same distance in every direction.

Oceans and Continents

Look at the map of the world. Some areas are coloured blue. The blue areas indicate water bodies and the other areas show land masses.

Very large land masses are known as **continents**. Very large water bodies are known as **oceans**.

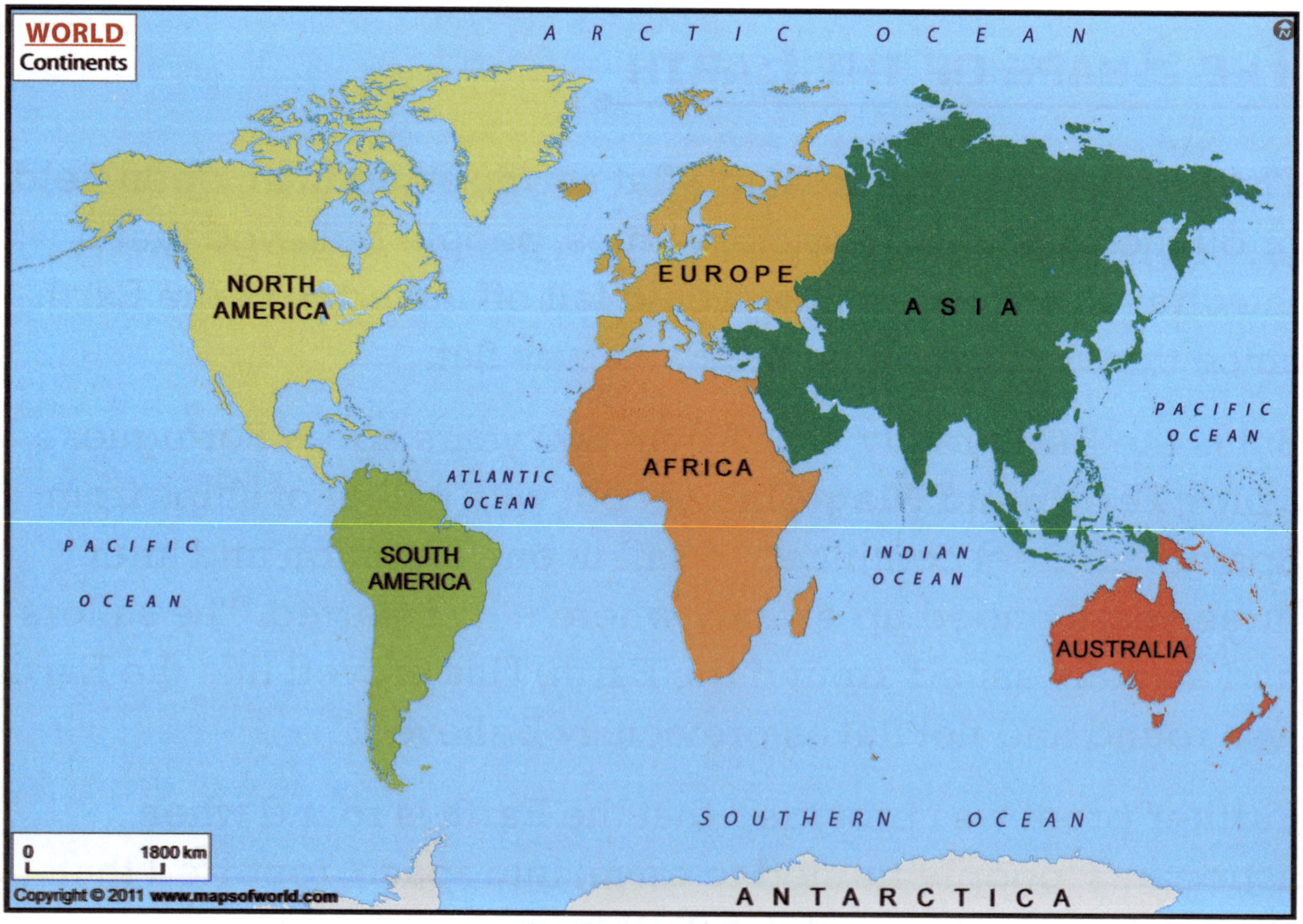

Continents and oceans

 ISBN 978-81-8477-937-0

There are seven continents in the world.

These are:

- Africa
- Asia
- Antarctica
- Australia
- Europe
- North America
- South America

Factastic

Australia is the smallest continent. Asia is the largest continent.

Continents are further divided into smaller divisions. These are known as **countries**. India is part of the continent of Asia.

Political map of the world

 ISBN 978-81-8477-937-0

Explore

Use an atlas to find the names of five countries that start with the letter A.

Circle Time

Play the word ladder game in class. Every student must come up with the name of an ocean, continent or country that starts with the same letter as the last letter of the word used by the student before him/her. For example, the ladder could be: Asia, Australia, Arctic Ocean, North America, etc.

Approximately 71 per cent of the Earth is covered with water, which is divided into oceans and seas. An ocean is a large body of saline (salty) water. There are five oceans in the world. These are:

- Arctic Ocean
- Atlantic Ocean
- Indian Ocean
- Pacific Ocean
- Southern Ocean

Factastic

The Southern Ocean is unique from the other oceans. All the other oceans are bordered by land on at least two sides. The Southern Ocean is the only ocean that does not have any land boundaries. Instead, it completely surrounds the continent of Antarctica.

The Southern Ocean came to be recognised only in the year 2000. Earlier, this area was considered the southern part of the Atlantic, Pacific and the Indian oceans.

Smaller bodies of water are known as **seas**. Oceans are very deep and are larger than seas. There are mountain ranges as well as trenches on the ocean floor. The **Mariana Trench**, located in the Pacific Ocean, is the deepest point on Earth.

 ISBN 978-81-8477-937-0

An **island** is a piece of land that is surrounded by water on all sides. Very often, islands are the tops of underwater mountains. A group of islands located close to one another is called an **archipelago.**

An archipelago is a group of islands

Explore

Use an atlas to find an archipelago in the Indian Ocean.

Learn More

On a world map, mark all the continents that surround the Indian Ocean. You may consult an atlas for this activity.

 ISBN 978-81-8477-937-0

Quiz Time

1. Find the names of the seven continents in the word grid.

X	Y	Z	X	Y	U	B	C	D	G	I	A
N	O	R	T	H	A	M	E	R	I	C	A
Z	U	W	A	V	X	E	F	H	I	J	K
L	P	Q	N	C	D	A	F	R	I	C	A
O	M	R	T	E	Q	Z	E	B	C	A	U
T	S	N	A	X	Z	M	D	E	F	R	S
U	X	Z	R	Y	A	S	E	I	H	Q	T
U	V	Q	C	H	S	R	U	J	G	P	R
A	C	W	T	L	I	Q	R	M	N	O	A
D	B	U	I	K	A	P	O	T	K	L	L
F	O	E	C	J	M	O	P	X	S	V	I
S	G	H	A	I	M	F	E	Y	W	U	A

 ISBN 978-81-8477-937-0

2. Fill in the blanks with the correct words from the brackets.

a. The __________ ____________ is the deepest point on Earth. (Mariana Trench/Marina Beach/Indian Ocean)

b. Very large masses of land are called ____________. (countries/states/continents)

c. There are ___________ continents in the world. (six/seven/eight)

d. ____________ is the largest continent in the world. (Africa/Australia/Asia)

e. There are ___________ oceans in the world. (seven/five/four)

3. Answer the questions.

a. What is the horizon?

b. How many oceans are there in the world?

c. India is part of which continent?

d. What is an archipelago?

4. On a physical map of the world, colour and label the following.

a. Africa

b. South America

c. Australia

d. Antarctica

e. Arctic Ocean

f. Atlantic Ocean

 ISBN 978-81-8477-937-0

4

INDIA—PHYSICAL

India is a large country. There are deserts, thick jungles and big rivers in India. It has a long coastline and beautiful beaches. Some of the tallest mountains in the world are located in India.

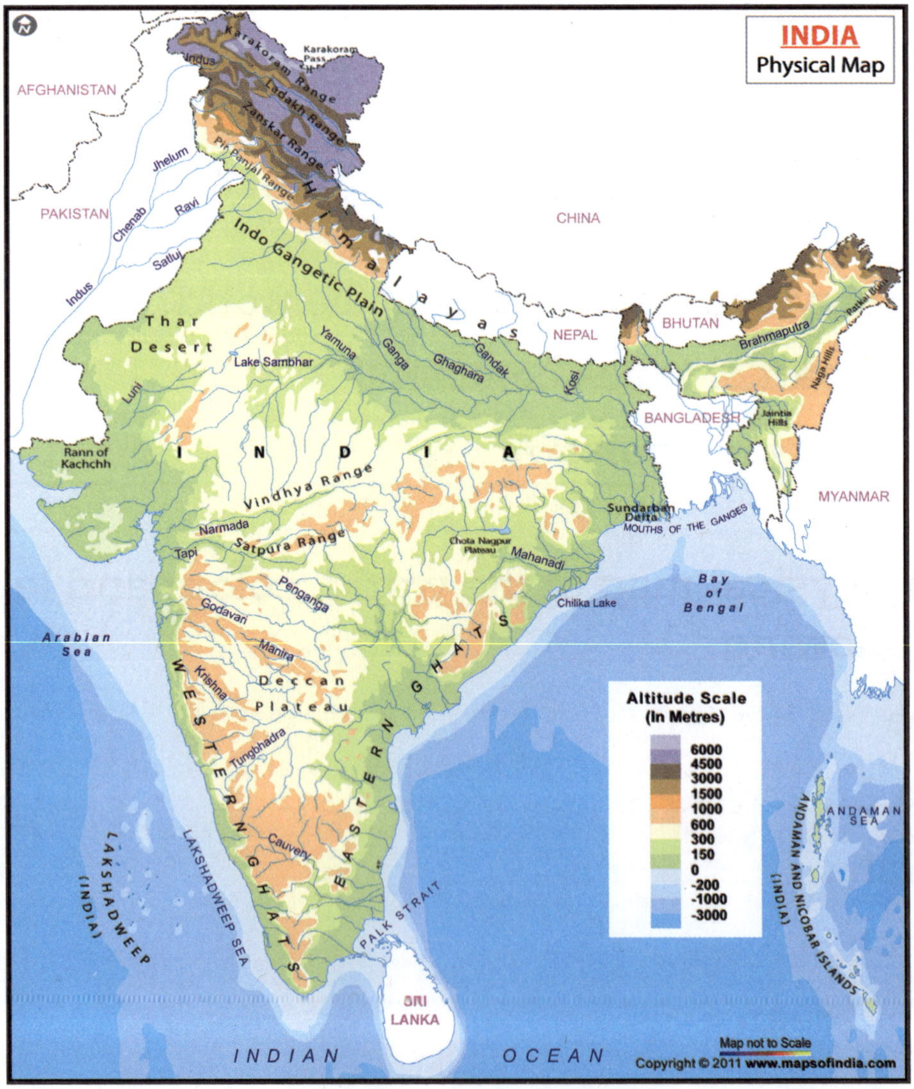

Physical map of India

 ISBN 978-81-8477-937-0

> **Factastic**
> India is the seventh-largest country in the world. It is also the second most populated country; the only country with more people than India is China. Both China and India are located in the continent of Asia.

India can be broadly divided into six geographical regions. These are:

- The Northern Mountains
- The Northern Plains
- The desert region
- The Deccan Plateau and the Ghats
- The coastal region
- The islands

Northern Mountains

The northern part of India has very high mountains called the **Himalayas**. A **mountain** is a portion of the Earth that rises steeply from the surrounding area. A chain of mountains is called a **range**.

The Himalayas are the world's highest mountain range. They form the northern boundary of India. It has some of the highest peaks in the world. These peaks are covered with snow throughout the year. **Mount Everest**, which is in Nepal, is the highest peak in the Himalayas. **Mount K2** is the second highest peak in the Himalayas.

Many important rivers of India, such as the Ganga, the Yamuna, the Indus and the Brahmaputra, start from the Himalayas. As the snow in the Himalayas starts to melt in spring, the rivers

ISBN 978-81-8477-937-0

swell up and flow down to the lower areas towards the plains and thick forests. This region, which has tall grass, is known as the **terai** region. Many animals live in the terai region, such as elephants, tigers, rhinoceros and deer.

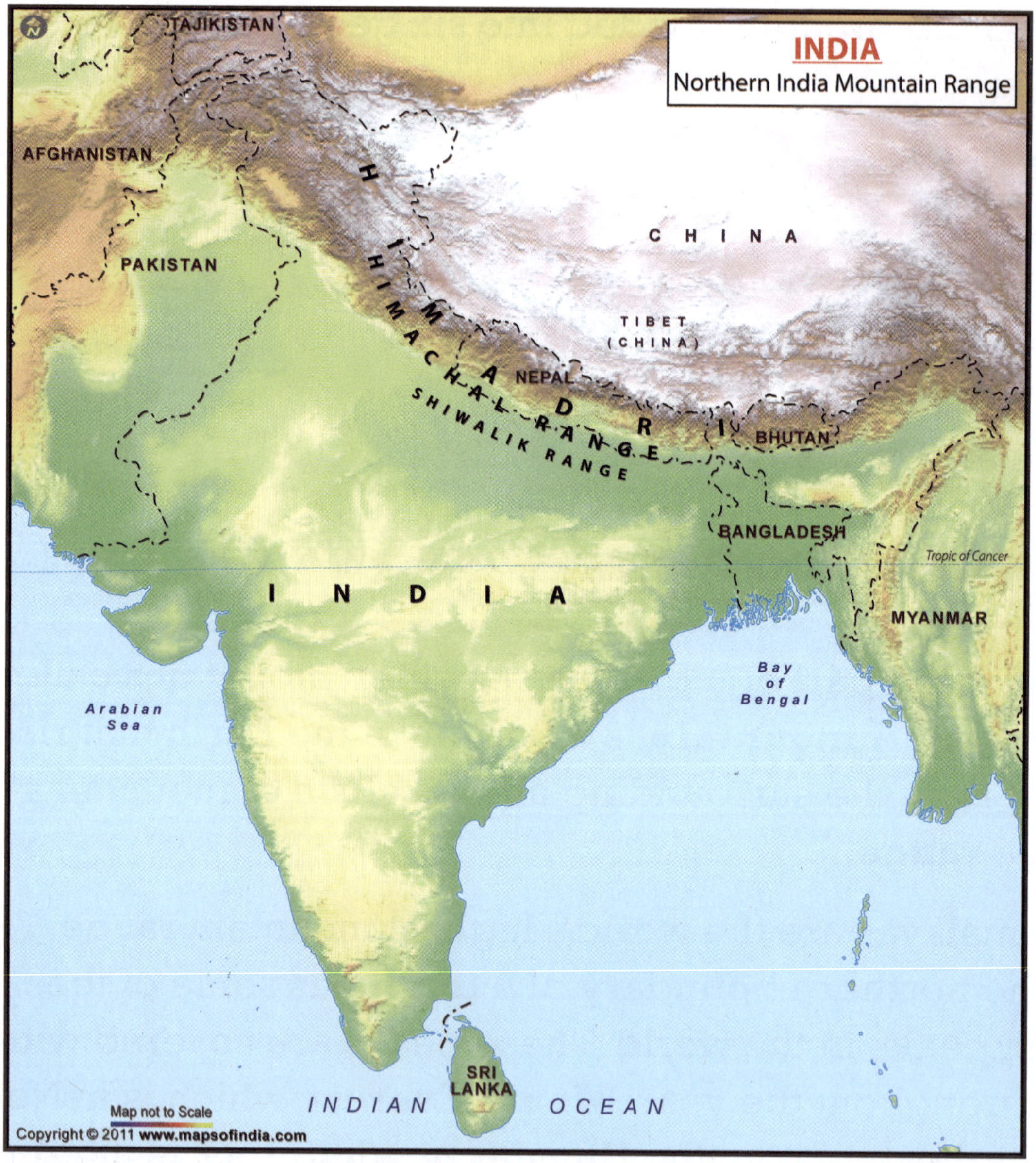

The Northern Mountains

Learn More

Find out where River Ganga originates.

 ISBN 978-81-8477-937-0

Explore

Find out who was the first person to climb to the peak of Mount Everest.

NORTHERN PLAINS

South of the Himalayas are the Northern Plains or the **Gangetic Plains**. These are flat lands with many rivers flowing through them. The rivers bring with them a fine soil known as **silt**, which makes the Northern Plains very fertile and most suitable for cultivation.

The Ganga flowing to the plains

The plains are very densely populated. Many well-known towns and cities are situated along the banks of the rivers that flow through this region. The plains are usually very hot in the summer and cold in winter.

DESERT

As we travel to the northwestern part of India, into the state of Rajasthan, the landscape changes. Here we find miles and miles of sand. This is known

A pack of camels in the Thar Desert

 ISBN 978-81-8477-937-0

as the **Great Indian Desert** or the **Thar Desert**. Since this region receives very little rainfall, hardly any crops grow here. This region experiences hot, dry summers and cold winters. The population in this region is very sparse as it is difficult to live in such extreme conditions.

Factastic

Villagers in Rajasthan depend on the camel as the main means of transport. Known as the **ship of the desert**, a camel can go without food and water for days together. It has wide cushioned feet that spread as it walks. This helps it to walk easily on sand and not slip. It also has two rows of eyelashes and nostrils that can close completely. This helps to prevent sand from entering the camel's eyes and nose.

Deccan Plateau and the Ghats

The southern part of India is a **peninsula**. A peninsula is a large piece of land jutting into the sea. It is surrounded by large water bodies on three sides. The Indian peninsula has the Bay of Bengal to the east, the Arabian Sea to the west and the Indian Ocean to the south.

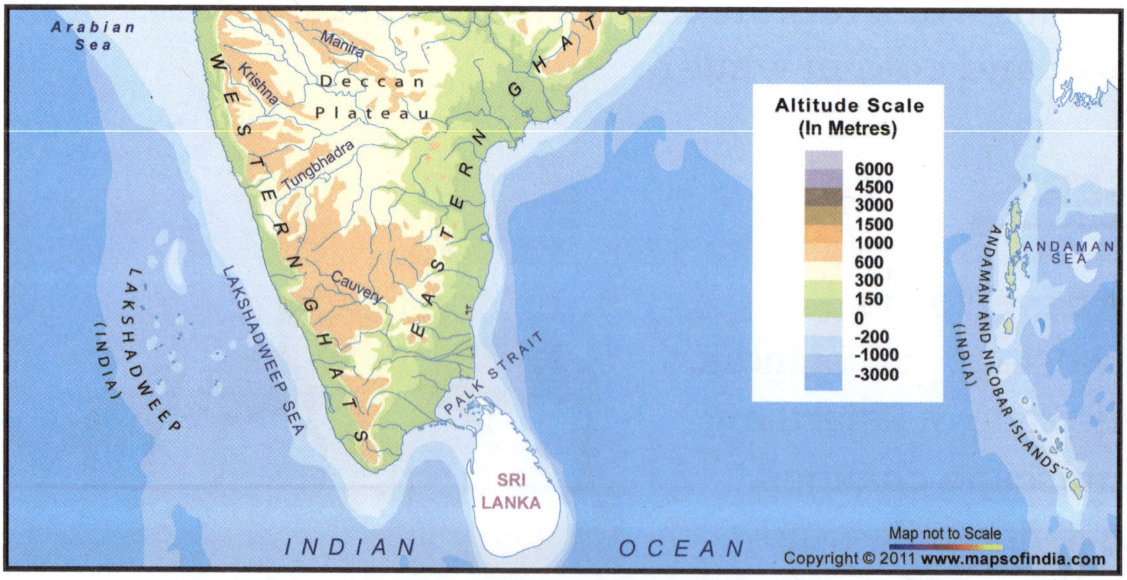

The Indian peninsula

 ISBN 978-81-8477-937-0

This region of India is called the **Deccan Plateau**. A **plateau** is a raised portion of land that is flat on top. The Deccan Plateau has many rivers, such as the Krishna, Kaveri, Godavari and Mahanadi, flowing through it. Unlike the rivers of the Northern Plains, the rivers in the Deccan Plateau are not snow fed but rain fed, that is, the source of water in the rivers of this region is rain water. The Deccan region is very rich in minerals. Some parts are covered by thick forests. The climate in the region is moderate, that is, it is neither too hot nor too cold. The Deccan Plateau is separated from the Northern Plains by two mountain ranges—the Satpuras and the Vindhyas.

Learn More

Use an encyclopedia or the Internet to find out the difference between the Eastern Ghats and the Western Ghats. Present your findings in a chart.

Coastal Regions

The Deccan Plateau is bordered on the east by a range of mountains called the **Eastern Ghats** and on the west by a range of mountains called the **Western Ghats**.

Narrow strips of land along the west coast and the east coast form the coastal regions of our country. The climate is neither too hot nor too cold. The Eastern Coastal Plain is broader than the Western Coastal Plain.

 ISBN 978-81-8477-937-0

ISLANDS

An island is a piece of land that is surrounded by water. India has many islands. The Andaman and Nicobar Islands are a group of islands in the Bay of Bengal. The Lakshadweep Islands are a group of islands in the Arabian Sea.

Learn More

Use an atlas to find out the capital cities of the Andaman and Nicobar Islands and Lakshadweep.

Quiz Time

1. Indicate whether the following statements are true (T) or false (F).

a. In India, the highest peaks are found in the plateaus. ☐

b. The Indus River originates in the Himalayas. ☐

c. The Eastern Coastal Plain is broader than the Western Coastal Plain. ☐

d. The Andaman Islands are in the Bay of Bengal. ☐

e. The Thar Desert is very densely populated because of its easy living conditions. ☐

2. Write three sentences on each of the following.

a. The Gangetic Plains

b. The Deccan Plateau

c. The Ghats

 ISBN 978-81-8477-937-0

3. Unscramble the letters to form words related to India's physical features.

a. YASMIHLAA ______________________________

b. HTAR SDEETR ______________________________

c. NWEETRS HGAST ______________________________

d. RVRIE AGNGA ______________________________

e. CADECN TEPLAUA ______________________________

4. Answer the questions.

a. What is a peninsula?

b. Name some rivers that start from the Himalayas.

c. Describe the Thar Desert.

d. Where is the terai region?

e. Which three large water bodies surround India?

5. On a physical map of India, mark the following.

a. Thar Desert

b. Himalayas

c. Deccan Plateau

d. Coastal regions

e. Andaman and Nicobar Islands

ISBN 978-81-8477-937-0

5

INDIA—POLITICAL

India is located in the southern part of the continent of Asia. India is surrounded by the Arabian Sea on the west, the Bay of Bengal on the east and the Indian Ocean to the south. Acting as a natural boundary, the Himalayas to the north separate India from the rest of the continent of Asia.

INDIA—NEIGHBOURS

India shares its boundaries with many countries. Bangladesh and Myanmar lie to its east. Sri Lanka and the Maldives are to the south of India. Pakistan and Afghanistan are India's neighbours in the west. China, Nepal and Bhutan lie to the north of our country. India and its neighbours form the Indian subcontinent.

India and her neighbours

subcontinent: a large land mass that is a part of a larger continent

 ISBN 978-81-8477-937-0

Explore

Use an atlas to find out the capitals of India's neighbours.

India's Political Divisions

India is a very large country with a large population. The central or union government looks after the needs, welfare and safety of the people of our country. The central government is located in New Delhi, which is the capital city. The Prime Minister, the President and other ministers of the central government live in New Delhi.

Factastic

People in India speak many different languages. About twenty-two regional languages are spoken in India.

As India is a large country, it is difficult for the central government to look after the needs of such a large population by itself. India has, therefore, been divided into twenty-eight states and eight union territories. Each state has a state government that looks after the well-being of all the people living in the state. The Governor, Chief Minister, other ministers and senior government officers of the state reside in the state capital.

Besides the states, there are eight union territories. These small areas come directly under the central government. Delhi is a union territory and is officially referred to as the National Capital Territory of Delhi. **Ladakh is the largest union territory by area** and **Lakshadweep is the smallest union territory by area**.

Hindi in Devanagari script is the official language of the Union government, while English is an associate official language for government work. India has no single national language, and states can choose their own official languages.

 ISBN 978-81-8477-937-0

People in the different parts of the country have diverse ways of dressing and living and have diverse eating habits. But despite this diversity, there is a sense of unity among the people of India.

India—States and Union Territories

 ISBN 978-81-8477-937-0

LIST OF STATES, UNION TERRITORIES AND THEIR CAPITALS

State	Capital
Andhra Pradesh	Amaravati
Arunachal Pradesh	Itanagar
Assam	Dispur
Bihar	Patna
Chhattisgarh	Raipur
Goa	Panaji
Gujarat	Gandhinagar
Haryana	Chandigarh
Himachal Pradesh	Shimla
Jharkhand	Ranchi
Karnataka	Bengaluru
Kerala	Thiruvananthapuram
Madhya Pradesh	Bhopal
Maharashtra	Mumbai
Manipur	Imphal
Meghalaya	Shillong
Mizoram	Aizawl
Nagaland	Kohima

I Care...

Every state in our country, whether big or small, is an important part of the country. We must treat all citizens of India with equal respect.

 ISBN 978-81-8477-937-0

State	Capital
Odisha	Bhubaneshwar
Punjab	Chandigarh
Rajasthan	Jaipur
Sikkim	Gangtok
Tamil Nadu	Chennai
Telangana	Hyderabad
Tripura	Agartala
Uttar Pradesh	Lucknow
Uttarakhand	Dehradun
West Bengal	Kolkata

Union Territory	Capital
Andaman and Nicobar Islands	Port Blair
Chandigarh	Chandigarh
Dadra and Nagar Haveli and Daman and Diu	Daman
Delhi (National Capital Territory)	New Delhi
Jammu and Kashmir	Srinagar (Summer), Jammu (Winter)
Ladakh	Leh
Lakshadweep	Kavaratti
Puducherry	Puducherry

Learn More

Which state/union territory do you live in? List the name of your state/union territory, the capital city and the name of the Chief Minister.

 ISBN 978-81-8477-937-0

Quiz Time

1. **Draw lines to match the states with their capitals.**

	State			Capital
a.	Uttar Pradesh	•	•	Bhubaneshwar
b.	Punjab	•	•	Kolkata
c.	Goa	•	•	Bengaluru
d.	Mizoram	•	•	Chandigarh
e.	Karnataka	•	•	Lucknow
f.	Odisha	•	•	Panaji
g.	West Bengal	•	•	Aizawl

2. **Fill in the blanks to complete the sentences.**

a. India's official languages are ________.

b. The ___________ range separates India from the rest of Asia.

c. India has __________ union territories.

d. India has __________ states.

e. India is located in the continent of __________.

3. **Answer the questions.**

a. Name India's neighbours.

b. Name the largest and the smallest union territories in India.

c. Where is the central government located?

 ISBN 978-81-8477-937-0

d. What is a subcontinent?

e. What is the difference between a state and a union territory?

4. The names of the capital cities of the following states are hidden in the grid. Can you spot them?

Goa Assam Arunachal Pradesh Jharkhand Madhya Pradesh Meghalaya Rajasthan Nagaland Bihar Maharashtra

S	M	U	M	B	A	I	W	L	I
D	Z	J	S	R	A	N	C	H	I
F	B	A	D	H	Q	Z	Q	K	T
S	H	I	L	L	O	N	G	Z	A
P	O	P	K	N	W	X	I	V	N
A	P	U	O	K	P	A	T	N	A
N	A	R	H	L	Y	K	K	X	G
A	L	O	I	I	U	M	L	V	A
J	Y	L	M	D	I	S	P	U	R
I	H	I	A	P	J	G	M	F	U

 ISBN 978-81-8477-937-0

6

India—Food and Clothing

India is a large country with diverse climate and weather conditions. The food and clothes of Indians vary, depending on where they live.

Food

Wheat

People across the country eat different kinds of food. The food that people eat in a particular region is known as the staple food of that region. The climate and the soil of that particular region influence the types of crops that can be grown there.

Rice

Rice grows best in regions where there is ample rain. It will not grow well in Rajasthan where there is very little rainfall and the soil is very sandy. This type of soil is very good for growing wheat, bajra and jowar.

 ISBN 978-81-8477-937-0

In the northern parts of the country, wheat is preferred over rice. *Gur* or jaggery is widely used.

Rice is the staple food of people living in the eastern and southern parts of India. In the coastal regions of India, fish is widely eaten.

Pulses are popular throughout the country.

Pulses

Fruits and vegetables are also a very important part of the Indian diet. Fruits and vegetables are available throughout the year.

Fruits require very specific weather and soil conditions to grow. Different fruits, therefore, grow in different parts of the country. Coconuts grow abundantly in the warm coastal areas of Tamil Nadu and Kerala. Large harvests of pineapple come from Assam, Goa and Kerala. There are several varieties of mangoes that are cultivated in India. The most famous of these are the Dussehri mango of Uttar Pradesh and the Alphonso mango of Ratnagiri, Maharashtra. Nagpur in Maharashtra is known as the Orange City because it is famous for its oranges. Himachal Pradesh and Ladakh produce a variety of apples. Jammu and Kashmir is famous for its apples, cherries and peaches.

Fruits

 ISBN 978-81-8477-937-0

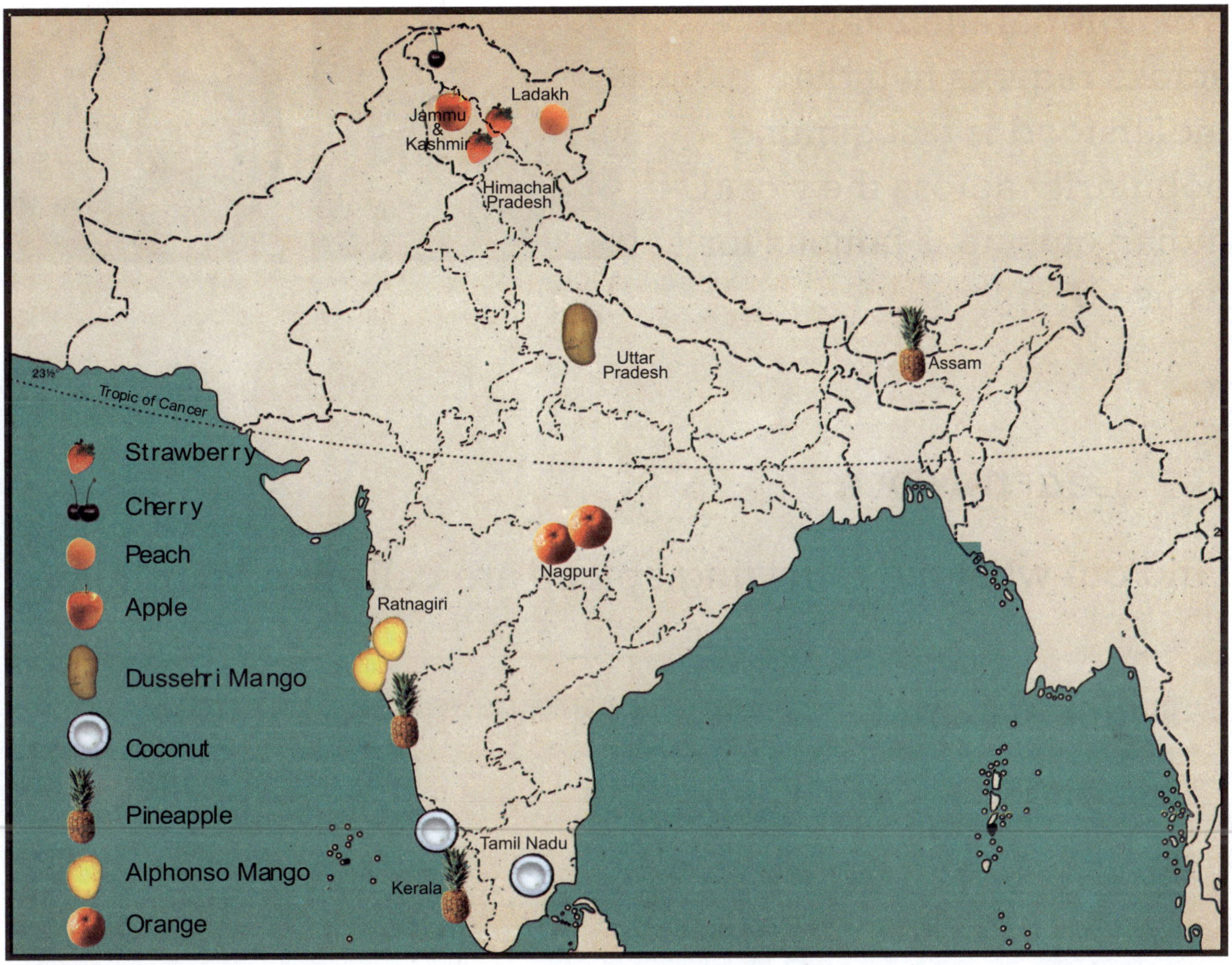

Fruits grown in India

Learn More

Name three items that vegetarians eat.
Name three items that non-vegetarians eat.

I Care...

We must never make fun of or show disgust at someone's food. We might not be familiar with a particular food item but it might be a special treat for someone else.

Explore

Mango is the national fruit of India. Use the Internet or an encyclopedia to find out the national fruit of any five nations. Present your findings in class.

 ISBN 978-81-8477-937-0

Food preparation varies across regions in India. Indian food is fast gaining popularity across the world. Indian cuisine is famous for its use of spices.

Learn More

Find out what the following spices are called in your home.

Spices	What they are called in your home
Turmeric	
Cloves	
Cinnamon	
Cardamom	
Coriander	

Spices add colour and flavour to food. Indian food is usually cooked in mustard oil, sunflower oil, sesame oil, groundnut oil or ghee (clarified butter).

Traditional Indian sweets are also very famous.

Circle Time

Which is your favourite Indian sweet? Find out how many students in your class like that sweet too.

 ISBN 978-81-8477-937-0

Clothing

People dress differently in different regions of the country. The clothes that people wear are influenced by the climate of that region.

India experiences a large variety of climatic conditions. The northern regions of our country, such as Leh and Ladakh, experience cold weather for most parts of the year. On the other hand, the southern states, such as Andhra Pradesh, Telangana and Tamil Nadu, are located near the Equator and experience warm equatorial weather for most parts of the year. People dress according to the weather that prevails. So people in Ladakh wear warm clothes for most parts of the year, while people in the warmer states of the south wear lighter cotton clothes for most parts of the year.

In general, we wear cotton clothes in summer to keep our bodies cool. In winter, we wear woollen clothes, such as shawls, scarves and sweaters, to keep our bodies warm. Synthetic or nylon clothes are worn in the rainy season. We also use umbrellas and raincoats in the monsoon.

Factastic

Mahatma Gandhi urged the people of India to wear khadi garments, which are a symbol of the Indian identity. According to Gandhiji, **khadi** is also the essence of **swadeshi**.

The most popular items of clothing among women in India are the saree and the salwar kameez, while most men in India wear kurta-pyjama or shirts and trousers.

khadi: any cloth that is hand spun or hand woven

 ISBN 978-81-8477-937-0

Each state and union territory also has its own distinct traditional wear. Here are a few examples of the traditional wear of the Indian states and union territories.

Andhra Pradesh

Arunachal Pradesh

Assam

Bihar

Chhattisgarh

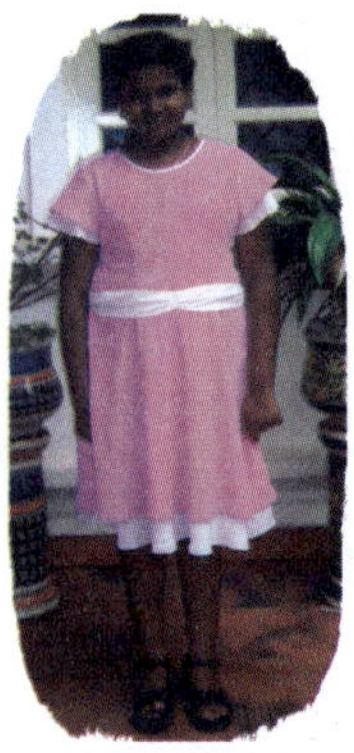
Goa

Gujarat

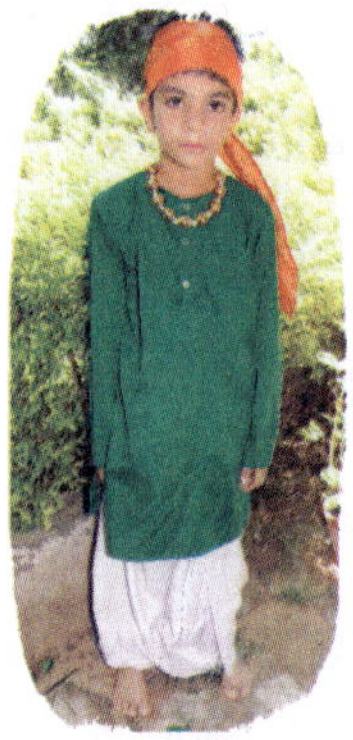
Haryana

Himachal Pradesh

Jammu and Kashmir

Jharkhand

Karnataka

Kerala

Madhya Pradesh

 ISBN 978-81-8477-937-0

Maharashtra

Manipur

Meghalaya

Mizoram

Nagaland

Odisha

Punjab

Rajasthan

Sikkim

Tamil Nadu

Tripura

Uttarakhand

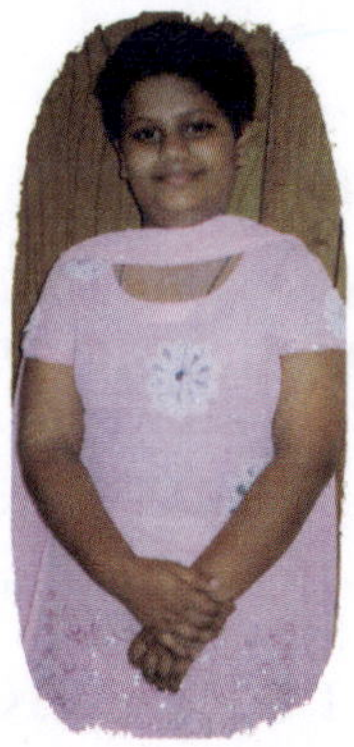
Uttar Pradesh

West Bengal

People wear traditional clothes on weddings as well as on special occasions.

Apart from traditional Indian clothes, men and women today also wear Western clothes, such as dresses, trousers, skirts and jeans.

 ISBN 978-81-8477-937-0

Quiz Time

1. Fill in the blanks with the correct words from the brackets.

a. In the northern parts of India, ______________ is preferred over rice. (wheat/pulses/fruits)

b. The _____________ is the most common piece of clothing worn by Indian women. (saree/jeans/pyjamas)

c. _____________ grows best in regions with high rainfall. (Rice/Wheat/Fruits)

d. ______________ grows in areas with low rainfall. (Bajra/Sugar cane/Rice)

e. People living in Leh and Ladakh wear ___________ clothes for most parts of the year. (cotton/woollen/nylon)

2. Indicate whether the following statements are true (T) or false (F).

a. We wear cotton clothes to keep us warm in winter. ☐

b. Clarified butter is known as ghee. ☐

c. In the northern part of India, bajra is the staple food. ☐

d. Leh and Ladakh experience warm tropical weather throughout the year. ☐

e. Gandhiji urged Indians to wear *khadi* garments. ☐

 ISBN 978-81-8477-937-0

3. **Draw lines to match the states and union territories listed in Column A with the fruits listed in Column B.**

	A			B
a.	Ladakh	•	•	Oranges
b.	Nagpur	•	•	Coconuts
c.	Ratnagiri	•	•	Cherries
d.	Jammu and Kashmir	•	•	Apples
e.	Kerala	•	•	Alphonso mangoes

4. **Answer the questions.**

a. What is a staple food?

b. Does rice grow in Rajasthan? Give reasons for your answer.

c. What are spices? Name any five.

d. Why do people in different parts of India eat different food?

e. What type of clothes do people wear in the summers?

f. Name two famous varieties of mangoes that grow in India.

5. **Why do you think people wear nylon and synthetic clothes in the rainy season?**

 ISBN 978-81-8477-937-0

7
Indian Culture and Tradition

India is a land of diverse cultures and traditions. A festival is a time for celebration. Festivals are an integral part of our cultural tradition and are celebrated for a number of reasons. While some festivals are common to the whole country, there are some that are celebrated only in some states. Some festivals are connected with religious events, while others are celebrated to usher in a particular season. In India, so many festivals are celebrated that not a single month goes by without a festival.

Let us discuss a few important Indian festivals.

Holi

Known as the festival of colours, Holi marks the end of winter and the onset of summer. Children play with water balloons and *pichkaris*. People throw coloured powder and water on each other and eat sweets such as *gujjias* and *malpuas*. The traditional drink served on Holi is *thandai*.

Holi is also associated with the puranic story of Holika, the sister of Hiranyakashyup, the demon-king. Holika had received

 ISBN 978-81-8477-937-0

a boon that she would remain safe even in a fire. The demon-king wanted to punish his son, Prahlad, who was a devotee of Lord Narayana. Prahlad was made to sit on Holika's lap in a pyre. When the pyre was lit, Holika was burned to ashes but Prahlad remained unharmed.

Factastic
Holi is celebrated with fervor in Mathura and Vrindavan. **Raaslila** or the divine dance is performed by the devotees of Lord Krishna.

Basant Panchami

Basant Panchami marks the beginning of spring or *basant*. It is celebrated mainly in Punjab and Haryana, when the mustard crops are in full bloom and the fields look like they are covered with a thick yellow blanket. People dress in shades of yellow and apply a *tika* on their foreheads.

Saraswati Puja

Saraswati Puja is performed on Basant Panchami in some states. Students seek the blessings of Saraswati—the goddess of learning—on this day. It is a tradition to fly kites, wear yellow clothes and prepare sweet yellow (or saffron) rice on Basant Panchami.

Factastic
Basant Panchami is celebrated on the fifth day of the Indian month of Maagh (January–February).

puranic story: story from one of the important Hindu religious texts
pyre: a large pile of wood for burning

 ISBN 978-81-8477-937-0

Raksha Bandhan

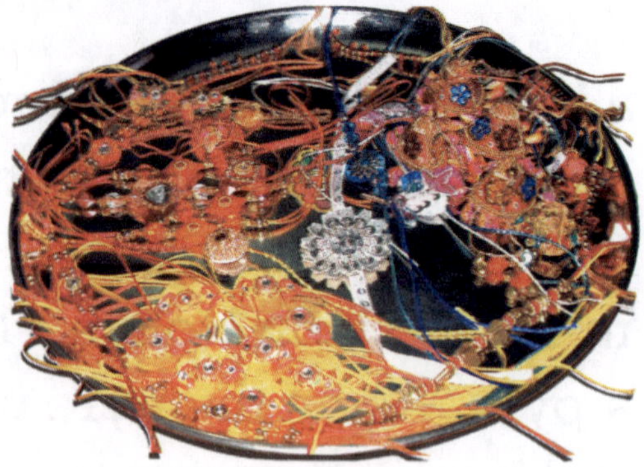

Rakhi

Raksha Bandhan means 'a bond of protection'. It is a festival that celebrates the bond between brothers and sisters. On this day, brothers promise to protect their sisters from harm. Sisters tie colourful *rakhis* around their brothers' wrists.

Raksha Bandhan falls on *Shravan Purnima*, usually in the month of August.

Dusshera

Dusshera is also known as Vijayadashmi. 'Vijay' means victory and 'Dashmi' means the tenth day. It marks the victory of good over evil, as it is believed that Lord Rama killed Ravana, the demon-king of Lanka, on this day. Ramlila is performed, enacting the battle between Lord Rama and Ravana. Effigies of Ravana, his brother Kumbhakarna and son Meghanad are burnt, symbolising the defeat of evil.

In West Bengal, Dusshera marks the end of **Durga Puja**.

Factastic

Navratri, the nine days preceding Vijayadashmi,are also celebrated in Gujarat. During Navaratri, men and women perform the *garba* and *rasa* dances.

Diwali

Diwali is celebrated eighteen days after Dusshera. It is known as the festival of lights. Oil lamps (popularly known as *diyas*) are lit and are used to decorate homes.

 ISBN 978-81-8477-937-0

In north India, Diwali marks Lord Rama's return to Ayodhya, after defeating the demon-king, Ravana.

People clean and decorate their homes on Diwali. They wear new clothes. In the evening, prayers are offered to Goddess Lakshmi—the goddess of wealth—following which *diyas* and candles are lit. People burst crackers and exchange sweets with their friends and relatives.

In West Bengal, this festival is associated with Goddess Kali.

GURUPURAB

Gurupurab is celebrated by Sikhs thrice a year to mark the birthdays of Guru Nanak Dev, Guru Gobind Singh and Guru Tegh Bahadur. Three days prior to Gurupurab, the **Guru Granth Sahib** is read continuously in gurudwaras. This is known as the *Akhand Path*. On the day of the festival, the holy book is decorated. People visit gurudwaras to offer prayers and eat *langar*.

Learn More

Find out what a *langar* is.

I Care...

Not everyone can afford new clothes and sweets to celebrate festivals. Donate toys, books and clothes to your city's orphanage.

Factastic

A few days before Gurupurab, early in the morning, processions (known as **Prabhat Pheris**) are taken out. In these processions, people sing hymns in praise of the gurus.

 ISBN 978-81-8477-937-0

Eid-ul-Fitr

Eid-ul-Fitr is celebrated by Muslims on the first day of Shawwal, marking the end of the holy month of Ramadan. During Ramadan, Muslims observe *roza*, a month-long fasting period. Eid, meaning festivity in Arabic, is celebrated after seeing the new crescent moon the previous evening. It is a time when Muslims give thanks for the blessings they have received from Allah. Families decorate their homes, gifts are given to friends and family, sweets and other delicacies are prepared, and new clothes are worn to celebrate the occasion.

Good Friday

Good Friday is the Friday of the Holy Week and marks the day Jesus was crucified. Many Christians spend this day praying and fasting.

It is believed that Jesus came back to life two days after Good Friday and visited his friends and followers again. This day is celebrated as **Easter**.

Christmas

Christmas is celebrated on 25 December every year, to celebrate the birth of Jesus Christ.

Factastic

Christmas trees are edible. Many parts of pines, spruces and firs, such as pollen, nuts and needles, can be eaten. The needles are a good source of vitamin C.

Shawwal: the tenth month of the Islamic calendar, following the month of Ramadan

 ISBN 978-81-8477-937-0

People decorate their homes with holly and Christmas trees, and exchange gifts with their friends and family. They also attend a special Christmas service at church.

Buddh Purnima

Buddh Purnima is celebrated to mark the birth of Lord Buddha. It was on this day that Lord Buddha attained enlightenment. Buddh Purnima is celebrated on a full moon day in the month of April or May.

Mahavir Jayanti

Mahavir Jayanti is a festival of the Jains. The birth of Lord Mahavir is celebrated on this day.

Navroz

Navroz celebrates the Parsi New Year. It is celebrated on or around 21 March. It marks the end of winter and the beginning of spring.

Bihu

Bihu is a harvest festival celebrated in the state of Assam. It is celebrated three times a year. Special songs and dances are performed and big bonfires lit to celebrate Bihu. Another important feature of Bihu celebrations are buffalo fights.

 ISBN 978-81-8477-937-0

Pongal

Pongal is a three-day harvest festival celebrated in Tamil Nadu. People decorate their homes and draw *kollams* in front of their home. A special dish called *pongal* is prepared using jaggery, newly harvested rice and milk to celebrate the festival.

Onam

The harvest festival of Kerala is called Onam. People wear new clothes and eat a special meal called the *onam sadya*. Decorated elephants are taken out in a procession during Onam. Another very special feature of this festival is the **snake boat race**. These are organised in different parts of Kerala during Onam.

Baisakhi

Baisakhi is the harvest festival of north India, especially Punjab and Haryana. Huge fairs are organised during Baisakhi. People don their traditional clothes and perform **bhangra** and **gidda** (a traditional dance for women) to the beat of the **dhol**.

Several other festivals are celebrated with great fervor in India, such as **Teej**, **Shivratri** and **Chhath**.

Learn More

Which is your favourite Indian festival? Draw a picture of your family and friends celebrating this festival. Write a few lines describing the festival and what you like most about it.

 ISBN 978-81-8477-937-0

DANCE

Indian dances and music signify celebrations offering thanks to the deities as well as a means of worship.

The diversity of Indian culture is reflected in the range of dance forms. Every region has a dance form specific to it. There are two types of dances—**classical** and **folk**.

In the olden days, classical dances were performed on special occasions and at a special place. But nowadays, these dances are performed on stage. The dancers train with *gurus* or teachers for several years.

Classical dancers wear colourful costumes and jewellery and use a lot of make-up when performing their dances.

In folk dances, the dancers do not necessarily have to be trained. Most folk dances involve a lot of footwork, body and hand movements along with facial expressions. They are performed solo or in groups.

Some classical dance forms of India

Kuchipudi from Andhra Pradesh

Bharatnatyam from Tamil Nadu

 ISBN 978-81-8477-937-0

Odissi from Odisha

Kathakali from Kerala

Some folk dances of India

Bhangra from Punjab

Angami dance from Nagaland

Cheraw or bamboo dance from Mizoram

Ghoomar from Haryana

Jhumur dance from Assam

 ISBN 978-81-8477-937-0

Folk dances are performed to celebrate a festival, the harvest season or to usher in a new season. They are usually accompanied by folk songs and musical instruments.

Learn More

Find out about other dance forms such as ballet, salsa and jazz.

Explore

Find out about any dance form popular in the state in which you reside. Make a chart on this art form and display it in class.

Music

Indian music includes a wide variety of folk, popular and classical forms. Music is a very important part of our heritage and is associated with religious traditions and other celebrations. Classical music includes Carnatic music (in the south) and Hindustani music (in the north).

Community singing is also an important part of Indian culture. People sing *bhajans* in temples, the *gurbani* in gurudwaras, hymns in church and *qawwalis* in *dargahs*.

Factastic

Classical music originated in the shlokas, chanted by priests while performing religious ceremonies.

 ISBN 978-81-8477-937-0

These are some of the musical instruments used in India.

Tabla

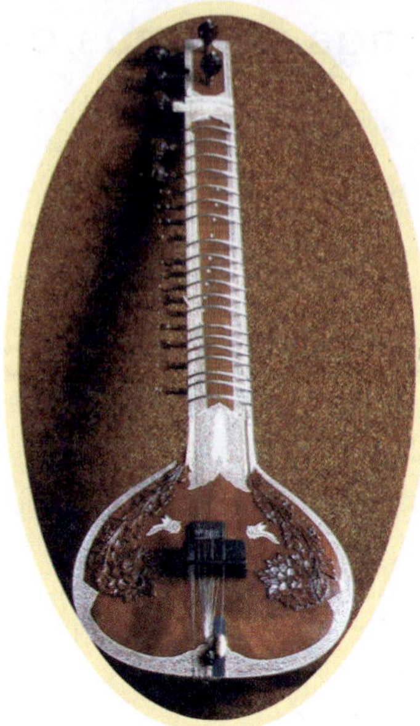

Sitar

Dholak

Veena

Sarangi

Santoor

Quiz Time

1. **Fill in the blanks with the correct words from the brackets.**

a. In West Bengal, __________ marks the end of Durga Puja. (Diwali/Holi/Dusshera)

b. Ghoomar is a folk dance from the state of __________. (Punjab/Haryana/Kerala)

 ISBN 978-81-8477-937-0

c. People sing ___________ in temples. (*bhajans*/ghazals/hymns)

d. The _______________ is the holy book of Sikhs. (Bible/Ramayana/Guru Granth Sahib)

e. __________ marks the onset of summer. (Diwali/Christmas/Holi)

2. **The names of some Indian dance forms and musical instruments have been given in jumbled form below. Unscramble the words.**

a. SSODII ____________________

b. RWCHEA ____________________

c. NAOOSTR ____________________

d. IIDUPCUHK ____________________

e. LABAT ____________________

f. RATIS ____________________

3. **Indicate whether the following statements are true (T) or false (F).**

a. The harvest festival of Tamil Nadu is called Onam. ☐

b. The dance form of Kuchipudi is native to Odisha. ☐

c. Navroz is celebrated on 25 December every year. ☐

d. The Cheraw dance is a folk dance of Mizoram. ☐

e. Eid-ul-Fitr is celebrated in the month of Ramadan. ☐

 ISBN 978-81-8477-937-0

4. Answer the questions.

a. Why are festivals celebrated?

b. Name a traditional food item made during Holi.

c. When is Eid-ul-Fitr celebrated?

d. What is the difference between classical and folk dances?

e. Name some harvest festivals celebrated in India.

5. Why are harvest festivals celebrated at different times in different parts of the country?

 ISBN 978-81-8477-937-0

8

National Symbols and Emblem

India is a land of diverse cultures and religions. Even though every region has different customs and traditions and we speak different languages, we are all Indians and belong to one country.

National Symbols

Symbols that represent a country are known as national symbols.

The **Royal Bengal tiger** is our national animal. It symbolises bravery and strength.

Royal Bengal tiger

Circle Time

The tiger is endangered in India because of poaching. Collect information about Project Tiger and tiger sanctuaries such as Ranthambore and Sundarbans. Have a discussion in class on what students can do to help protect the tiger.

 ISBN 978-81-8477-937-0

Our national bird is the **peacock**. It is famous for its beauty and unusual feathers. It symbolises grace, pride and beauty.

Peacock

Lotus

The **lotus** is India's national flower. It is an aquatic plant that grows in shallow water. Despite growing in a muddy environment, it always appears clean and beautiful. The lotus flower symbolises purity, wealth and knowledge.

Explore

Apart from India, the lotus is the national flower of another Asian nation. Use the Internet or an encyclopedia to find out the name of this country.

The **banyan** tree is India's national tree. It is considered a sacred tree.

Banyan tree

The **mango** is India's national fruit. It has been cultivated in India since time immemorial. There are over a hundred varieties of mangoes in India, in a range of colours, sizes and shapes. In India, we eat mangoes ripe, or prepare pickles and chutneys from raw ones.

Mango

 ISBN 978-81-8477-937-0

Learn More

Draw the logo or symbol of your school.

Our National Flag

The national flag is the symbol of the freedom and unity in our country. Our national flag is rectangular in shape and consists of three colours. It is, therefore, referred to as the tricolour or the *tiranga*. It has a deep saffron (*kesaria*) band at the top, a white band in the middle and a green band at the bottom. There is a navy blue wheel or *Dharma Chakra* in the middle of the white band.

The saffron colour stands for the strength and courage of India. The white stands for peace, and the green stands for growth and prosperity. The chakra has twenty-four spokes representing the hours of the day. It symbolises constant effort and growth.

> **Factastic**
>
> The **Dharma Chakra**, also known as the Ashoka Chakra, depicts the wheel of law. It has been adapted from the Sarnath Lion Capital, which was built in the third century BCE during the reign of the Mauryan emperor Ashoka.

The national flag can be hoisted at home, in school and in offices keeping in mind these rules:

- The saffron band must always be at the top.
- No other flag can be placed above the tricolour.
- The flag must be taken down from the flag pole before sunset and folded carefully.
- We must always respect and honour our national flag.

 ISBN 978-81-8477-937-0

Our National Anthem

Our national anthem, *Jana Gana Mana*, was written by Rabindranath Tagore. The original poem has five stanzas, but only the first stanza is sung as the national anthem.

The national anthem is played or sung on national holidays, public functions and at international events.

India's national anthem

Jana-gana-mana-adhinayaka, jaya he
Bharata-bhagya-vidhata
Punjab-Sindh-Gujarata-Maratha-
Dravida-Utkala-Banga
Vindhya-Himachala-Yamuna-Ganga
Uchchala-Jaladhi-taranga
Tava shubha name jage
Tava shubha ashish mage
Gahe tava jaya-gatha
Jana-gana-mangala-dayaka jaya he
Bharata-bhagya-vidhata
Jaya he, jaya he, jaya he
Jaya jaya jaya, jaya he!

Factastic

It takes about fifty-two seconds to sing our national anthem. The national anthem of Bangladesh is also a poem penned by Rabindranath Tagore.

 ISBN 978-81-8477-937-0

Our national song is *Vande Mataram*. It was composed in Sanskrit by Bankim Chandra Chatterji. It was inspired by the freedom struggle.

Our National Emblem

The Sarnath Lion Capital

Our national emblem has been adapted from the Sarnath Lion Capital, built by Ashoka in Uttar Pradesh.

The original Sarnath Lion Capital has four lions, standing back to back, mounted on an abacus. The emblem shows only three lions (the fourth is hidden from view). The wheel below it has an elephant, a galloping horse, a bull and a lion over a bell-shaped lotus.

The words *Satyameva Jayate* from the **Mundaka Upanishad** are written in the **Devanagari** script below the abacus. *Satyameva Jayate* means 'Truth Alone Triumphs'.

Learn More

Find out which is the national sport of India. Make a chart describing the sport.

I Care...

As a mark of respect to our nation, we must always stand in attention whenever the national anthem is being played or sung.

 ISBN 978-81-8477-937-0

Quiz Time

1. Fill in the blanks to complete the following sentences.

a. India's national fruit is ____________.

b. The Indian flag is ____________ in shape.

c. In the Indian flag, the colour white stands for ____________.

d. The original Sarnath Lion Capital has ____________ lions.

e. ____________ is India's official language.

2. Indicate whether the following statements are true (T) or false (F).

a. The words *Satyameva Jayate* mean 'Truth Alone Triumphs'. ☐

b. India's national animal is the Royal Bengal tiger. ☐

c. The saffron band in the Indian flag symbolises prosperity. ☐

d. One must stand in attention when the national anthem is being played. ☐

e. India's national song is *Jana Gana Mana*. ☐

3. Answer the questions.

a. Describe the Indian national emblem.

b. What is the *Dharma Chakra*?

c. What are national holidays? How are they different from religious festivals?

d. Describe India's flag.

 ISBN 978-81-8477-937-0

9

New Delhi

New Delhi is the capital of India. It is known as the **National Capital Territory (NCT)**. It lies on the western banks of River Yamuna. It shares its borders with the states of Haryana and Uttar Pradesh. Delhi consists of two cities—New Delhi and Old Delhi. It is one of the fastest growing cities in India.

History

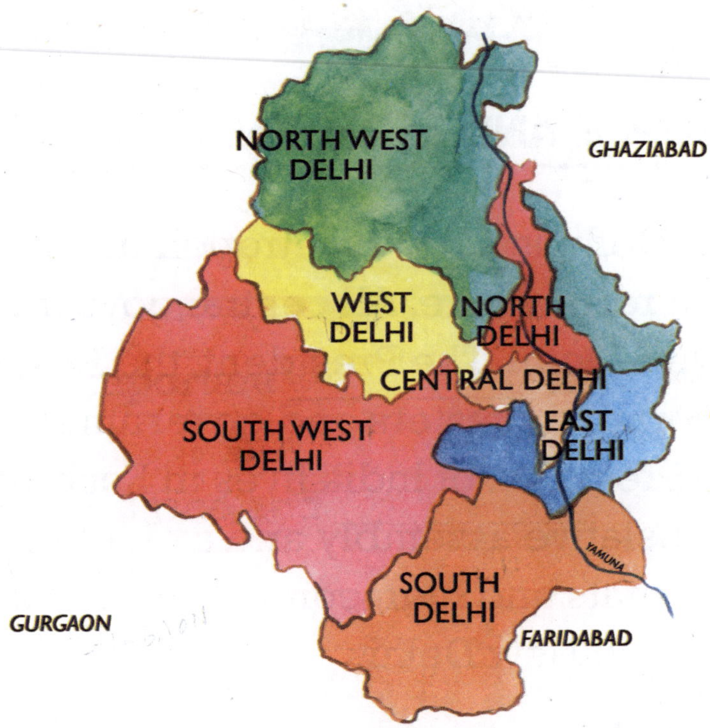

Delhi became the capital of modern India in 1947 when India gained independence. Delhi has always played an important role in the history of India. Some people came to India as migrants and others as invaders only to settle in the city. They brought with them their language, customs, culture and art. The Mughals as well as the British left a deep impact on the city.

migrants: people who move from place to place in search of seasonal work
invaders: people who enter a country in a large group, such as an army, in order to occupy and rule

 ISBN 978-81-8477-937-0

The modern city of Delhi contains the remnants of several ancient cities. These are: Quila Rai Pithora, Firozabad, Shahjehanabad, Mehrauli, Shergarh, Tughlakabad, Jahapanah, Indraprastha and Siri.

The National Capital Region (NCR) of Delhi is an area comprising Old Delhi, New Delhi, Delhi cantonment and few towns spread over neighbouring states such as Alwar (Rajasthan), Gurgaon (Haryana), Noida and Ghaziabad (Uttar Pradesh).

Factastic

Planned by Edwin Lutyens, a leading twentieth-century British architect, New Delhi is known for its wide, tree-lined roads, numerous national institutions and landmarks.

People and Government

New Delhi is a truly metropolitan city. People from all parts of India reside here. All central government offices are located in New Delhi. The President, the Prime Minister and many important ministers and government officials also live here. The President of India lives in Rashtrapati Bhawan. Delhi has a legislative assembly and a chief minister. Ambassadors, diplomats and high commissioners of various countries also reside in New Delhi.

I Care...

The Delhi Metro has promised to plant 10,000 saplings to replace the trees felled during the construction of the metro. We need to take care of our environment and ensure that the green cover of our cities are maintained.

metropolitan: of or pertaining to a large city, its surrounding suburbs, and other neighbouring communities
legislative assembly: a group having legislative or law-making powers
ambassadors: diplomats sent by countries as their representatives in foreign countries

 ISBN 978-81-8477-937-0

Climate

Delhi experiences extreme climatic conditions. During the summer months, it is very hot. The summers stretch from April to October. Hot winds known as *loo* blow during peak summer, sometimes accompanied by dust storms as well. Monsoon is moderate while winters are very cold.

Industries

Delhi is a big commercial centre. Information technology, banking, manufacturing, leather processing and pharmaceuticals are some of the major industries of this region.

Tourist Attractions

There are many places popular with tourists in Delhi.

Rajpath is an important road in central Delhi. This is where the Republic Day parade is held. At the eastern end of Rajpath is the **India Gate** while at the western end is the **Rashtrapati Bhawan**.

India Gate is a stone memorial built in the memory of soldiers who lost their lives in World War I. It is 42 m high. The Amar Jawan Jyoti burns at the India Gate in memory of these Indian soldiers.

India Gate

Rashtrapati Bhawan, the official residence of the President of India, is situated on Raisina Hill. It was designed by Edward Lutyens. It is the largest

 ISBN 978-81-8477-937-0

residence of any head of state in the world. It is also very famous for its Mughal Gardens, which are open to the public every year in February.

The **Red Fort**, also known as the **Lal Quila**, was built by the Mughal Emperor, Shah Jahan. It took ten years to build it. The sound and light show, narrating the history of India, takes place at the fort every day. Every year on 15 August, the Prime Minister hoists the flag at the Red Fort.

Red Fort

> **Factastic**
> The Mughal Emperor Shah Jahan (popular for building the Taj Mahal of Agra) transferred his capital from Agra to Delhi. The Red Fort was completed in 1648, nine years after the emperor shifted to this city.

Learn More

Imagine you are the Prime Minister of the country. You have to address the nation on the occasion of Independence Day. Prepare a five-minute speech and present it in class.

Raj Ghat

Close to the Red Fort, on the banks of the Yamuna River, is the **Raj Ghat**. It is a memorial for Mahatma Gandhi and was built shortly after his assassination in 1948.

> **assassination:** the action of murdering (an important person) for political or religious reasons

 ISBN 978-81-8477-937-0

The **Jama Masjid** is the largest mosque in India. It was built by Shah Jahan in Delhi in 1650. The construction of the mosque took six years.

Jama Masjid

Qutab Minar

Qutab-ud-din Aibak started the construction of the **Qutab Minar**, the world's tallest minaret. Located in the same complex as the Qutab Minar is an iron pillar that is nearly 7 m (approx 22.96 feet) high. What makes this pillar unique is that it shows no signs of rusting though it is built in an open area.

Other places of interest in Delhi include the Baha'i Lotus Temple, Jantar Mantar, Lodi Garden, Humayun's Tomb, Nehru Planetarium, Gurudwara Bangla Sahib, St. James Church and Chandni Chowk, which is a very busy market located opposite the Red Fort.

Delhi is also famous for the metro—a rapid transit system serving Delhi, Gurgaon, Noida and Ghaziabad.

The Indira Gandhi International Airport in Delhi is the busiest airport in India. With the commencement of operations at the new Terminal 3, it has become South Asia's largest aviation hub.

In 2010, Delhi hosted the XIX Commonwealth Games. Seventy-one Commonwealth nations and dependencies competed in twenty-one sports to make it the largest Commonwealth Games to date.

 ISBN 978-81-8477-937-0

Explore

Collect pictures of important tourist attractions in Delhi and make a collage.

Quiz Time

1. Indicate whether the following statements are true (T) or false (F).

a. New Delhi is the national capital of India. ☐

b. River Ganga flows through Delhi. ☐

c. The largest mosque in Delhi is the Jama Masjid. ☐

d. The mosques and forts in Delhi were built during the British rule. ☐

e. The climate of Delhi is moderate. ☐

f. Delhi became the capital of modern India in 1947. ☐

2. Answer the questions.

a. What is the official residence of the President of India called?

b. What is NCR?

c. What is the climate of Delhi like?

d. What is the importance of India Gate?

 ISBN 978-81-8477-937-0

3. Use the clues to solve the crossword.

ACROSS

4 Mahatma Gandhi's memorial

5 A famous mosque in Delhi

6 The Amar Jawan Jyoti burns here

7 A monument made of red sandstone

DOWN

1 A famous market opposite the Red Fort

2 A tall minaret in Delhi

3 A Baha'i temple in the shape of our national flower

 ISBN 978-81-8477-937-0

10
MUMBAI

Mumbai, the capital of Maharashtra, is situated on the west coast of India by the Arabian Sea. Mumbai was earlier known as Bombay. The name of the city was officially changed in 1995. It is one of the most populated cities in the world, with a population of about 30 million people. It is the commercial and entertainment hub of India. It is considered to be India's economic capital.

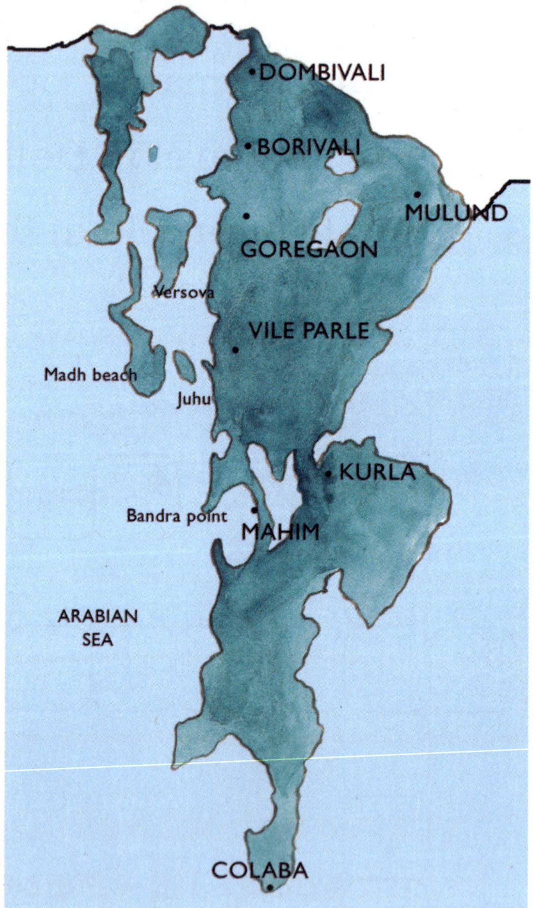

The Governor, Chief Minister and cabinet ministers of Maharashtra reside in Mumbai.

Mumbai consists of two distinct areas: the town and the suburbs. The town region is commonly known as the Island City.

Factastic

The name Mumbai is derived from Mumba—the name of the Hindu goddess Mumbadevi. It is sometimes still referred to by its older names, like Kakamuchee and Galajunkja.

 ISBN 978-81-8477-937-0

History

Mumbai originally consisted of seven islands. Around 300 years ago, they were occupied by the Koli fisherfolk. This group of islands, which have since been joined together by a series of reclamations, formed part of the kingdom of Ashoka, the famous emperor of India. They were initially ruled by the Hindus and later by the Muslims, followed by the Portuguese. Finally, the British Crown took control of the islands in the 1660s.

> **Factastic**
> Mumbai played an important role in the freedom struggle. Mahatma Gandhi lived in this city for several years.

Climate

> **Factastic**
> The highest rainfall recorded in recent times in Mumbai in a single day was 944 millimeters (37.17 in) on 26 July 2005.

Since Mumbai is located next to the sea, it has warm, humid summers and pleasant winters. Between March and October, humidity is very high and the temperature ranges between 30°C to 35°C. During the monsoons, in June, July and August, it receives heavy rainfall.

Industries and Institutions

Mumbai has many factories that make textiles, medicines, oils, chemicals and electronic goods.

India's most important petroleum field is situated at Bombay High, off the Mumbai coast. Being the largest port of India, Mumbai plays an important role in the import–export industry.

 ISBN 978-81-8477-937-0

Other important institutions in Mumbai are the Bhabha Atomic Research Centre (BARC), the Tata Institute of Fundamental Research (TIFR) and the Indian Institute of Technology (IIT).

Factastic

In 1853, the British built the first railway line from Mumbai to Thane.

Tourist Attractions

There are many places popular with tourists in Mumbai.

Gateway of India

The **Gateway of India** is one of the main tourist attractions of the city. It was built to commemorate the visit of King George V and Queen Mary to Bombay in 1911.

Marine Drive, also known as the Queen's Necklace, looks splendid when illuminated at night.

Chhatrapati Shivaji Terminus

 ISBN 978-81-8477-937-0

Juhu and **Girgaum Chowpatty** are two of the many beaches that are famous in Mumbai.

Another famous building is the **Chhatrapati Shivaji Terminus**, which is a railway terminus.

Other places of interest in Mumbai are the **Prince of Wales Museum**, the **Nehru Planetarium**, the **National Science Centre**, the **Hanging Gardens**, **Essel World** and the **Taraporevala Aquarium**.

The Hindi film industry, Bollywood, is a very important part of Mumbai.

The Chhatrapati Shivaji International Airport is one of the busiest airports in India.

The Rajiv Gandhi Sea Link, a cable stayed bridge over the Arabian Sea, was inaugurated in 2009. It links Bandra to Worli.

Learn More

Find out what festivals are celebrated in Mumbai. Make a chart or a file about these festivals.

Mumbai is famous for its *bhel puri*, *pav bhaji*, *vada-pav* and *srikhand*.

Explore

Find out information about Taj Mahal Palace Hotel. Why was it in the news some years back?

 ISBN 978-81-8477-937-0

Quiz Time

1. **Fill in the blanks with the correct words from the brackets.**

a. Mumbai was earlier known as ____________________.
(Calcutta/Bombay/Madras)

b. ____________________ is a famous beach in Mumbai.
(Chowpatty/Bombay High/Marine Drive)

c. The Hindi film industry is called ____________________.
(Hollywood/Bollywood/Tollywood)

d. ____________________ International Airport is in Mumbai.
(Chhatrapati Shivaji/Indira Gandhi/Victoria Terminus)

e. Mumbai is the capital of ____________________.
(Gujarat/Goa/Maharashtra)

2. **Give one-word answers for the following.**

a. Name one food item Mumbai is famous for.

b. Name an important train station in Mumbai.

c. Name one famous beach in Mumbai.

d. Give another name for the 'Queen's Necklace'.

e. Name Mumbai's international airport.

 ISBN 978-81-8477-937-0

3. Draw lines to match the dates listed in Column A with the events listed in Column B.

	A		B
a.	1996 •		• The Gateway of India was built
b.	1660s •		• Name changed to Mumbai
c.	1911 •		• Highest rainfall recorded
d.	1853 •		• British took control of the islands
e.	2005 •		• The first railway line was constructed in Mumbai

4. Answer the questions.

a. Why was the Gateway of India built?

b. Write a short note on the history of Mumbai.

c. Name some important institutions in Mumbai.

d. Describe Mumbai's climate.

 ISBN 978-81-8477-937-0

11
Kolkata

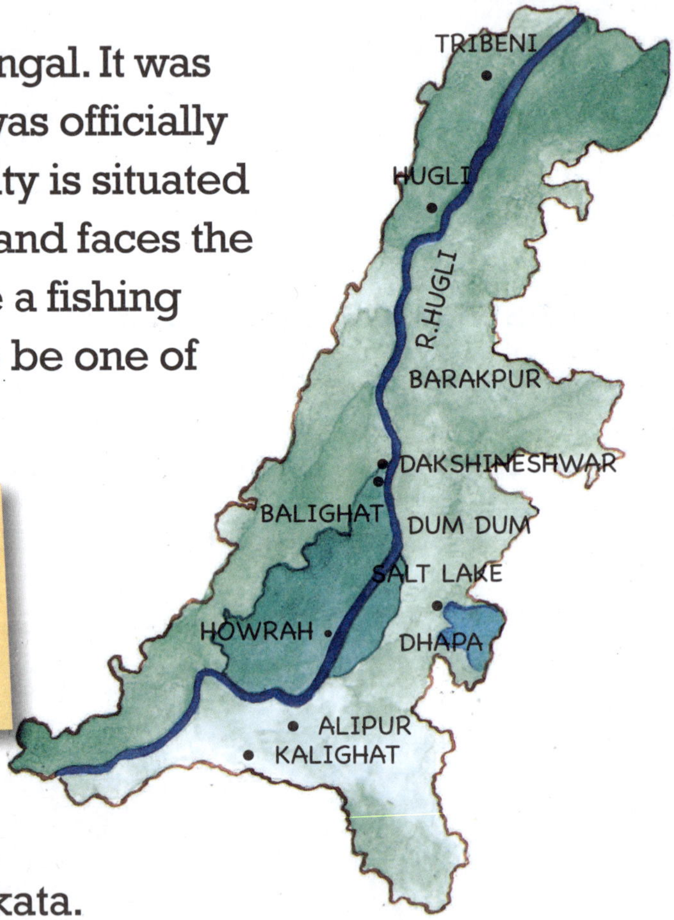

Kolkata is the capital of West Bengal. It was known as Calcutta earlier and was officially renamed Kolkata in 2001. The city is situated on the banks of the River Hugli and faces the Bay of Bengal. Kolkata was once a fishing village, which has now grown to be one of India's most populated cities.

Factastic
Calcutta was the capital of British India until 1911 and was once referred to as 'the city of palaces'.

The offices of the West Bengal government are located in Kolkata. The Governor, the Chief Minister, other ministers and government officials live in the city.

History

The history of Kolkata is not as old as that of Delhi. Calcutta was established by the British in 1690. It was formed by joining together the three villages of Sutanuti, Gobindapur and Kalikata.

 ISBN 978-81-8477-937-0

Climate

Like Mumbai, Kolkata also experiences warm and humid summers. As it lies in the eastern part of India, it receives heavy rainfall during the monsoon season. The winters are cool.

Industries and Institutions

Diamond Harbour is an important port in Kolkata. The main railway station is called Howrah Station. Kolkata's airport is named the Netaji Subhash Chandra Bose Airport.

> **Factastic**
> The old hanging bridge on the River Hugli, known as the Rabindra Setu, connects Kolkata and Howrah. It is popularly known as the Howrah Bridge.

Rice, rubber, jute, textile, chemical and paper are some of the important industries in Kolkata.

Tourist Attractions

Kolkata attracts many tourists every year.

Some of the places popular with tourists are:

- Fort William
- The Victoria Memorial (famous for its statues and paintings)
- The Botanical Garden (known for its ancient banyan trees)
- The Indian Museum

Victoria Memorial

 ISBN 978-81-8477-937-0

- Alipore Zoo
- Birla Planetarium
- Ramakrishna Mission at Belur Math
- Eden Gardens
- Salt Lake Stadium
- The National Library (the biggest library in India)
- St. Paul's Cathedral

St. Paul's Cathedral

I Care...

People of many different religions call Kolkata their home. Muslims, Christians, Jews, Hindus, Jains and Buddhists have lived together in Kolkata for many years and there have never been any problems between any of these communities. We must respect all religious communities and live harmoniously with each other.

Factastic

Bengali is the main language spoken in Kolkata. Hindi and English are also very popular.

Learn More

What are the Eden Gardens famous for?

Food

The staple diet of the Bengalis is rice and fish. The sweets that Kolkata is famous for are *sandesh*, *rasogulla* and *mishti doi*.

Kolkata has a very rich and diverse culture. People are fond of dancing, singing, poetry and painting.

The most popular games in Kolkata are football and cricket.

 ISBN 978-81-8477-937-0

Explore

Find out about the main festivals celebrated in Kolkata.

Factastic

The underground railway system, known as the Metro, is another tourist attraction. It connects the northern and the southern parts of the city.

Explore

There is a mode of public transport that is found only in Kolkata and not in any other Indian city. Find out which mode of transport this is.

Quiz Time

1. Fill in the blanks with the correct words from the brackets.

a. Diamond Harbour is an important __________ in Kolkata. (bridge/station/port)

b. The staple diet of Bengal is rice and __________. (meat/fish/*sandesh*)

c. Most people in Kolkata speak __________. (Bengali/Urdu/Hindi)

d. Kolkata is the capital of __________. (New Delhi/Andhra Pradesh/West Bengal)

e. Calcutta was established by the __________. (Dutch/Portuguese/British)

 ISBN 978-81-8477-937-0

2. Draw lines to match the following.

a.	River	•	• Banyan trees
b.	Railway station	•	• Howrah
c.	Bridge	•	• Hugli
d.	Sweet	•	• Rabindra Setu
e.	Botanical Garden	•	• *Sandesh*

3. Give one-word answers for the following.

a. Name the biggest library in India.

b. What is Kolkata's underground railway system known as?

c. Apart from cricket, which sport is very popular in Kolkata?

d. In which year was the city of Calcutta established?

e. In which year was the name of the city changed from Calcutta to Kolkata?

4. Answer the questions.

a. Describe the climate of Kolkata.

b. What are the major industries of Kolkata?

c. List five tourist attractions of Kolkata.

d. Name the villages that were joined to form the city of Kolkata.

 ISBN 978-81-8477-937-0

12
CHENNAI

Chennai is the capital of Tamil Nadu. It was formerly known as Madras. It was renamed in 1996. It is the fourth-largest metropolitan city of India. Located on the Coromandel Coast of the Bay of Bengal, it has attracted many traders and merchants.

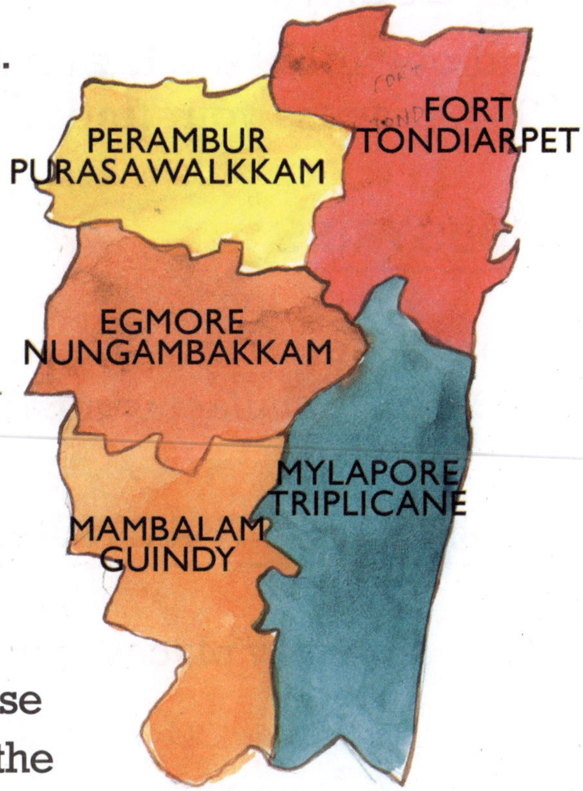

HISTORY

In the sixteenth century, the Portuguese traders came to this city, followed by the Dutch and the British.

The name Chennai is derived from Chennapattinam, the name of the town that grew around Fort St. George, which was built by the British in 1640.

Factastic
The Marina Beach stretches over a distance of about 12 km.

CLIMATE

Chennai lies near the Equator and on the coast, which prevents extreme variation in seasonal temperature. For most of the

 ISBN 978-81-8477-937-0

year, the weather is hot and humid. The city gets most of its seasonal rainfall from the northeast monsoon winds, from mid-September to mid-December. Cyclones in the Bay of Bengal sometimes hit the city.

Learn More

Find out about the tsunami that hit the coast of Chennai in 2004. Discuss your findings in class.

INDUSTRIES

Chennai's economy is based on the automobile, technology, hardware manufacturing and healthcare industries.

TOURIST ATTRACTIONS

There are many places that are popular with tourists in Chennai. They are:

- Fort St. George (houses the secretariat and the legislative assembly)
- The St. Thomas Church
- St. Mary's Church (built by the British in 1680)
- The Santhome Basilica

Santhome Basilica

 ISBN 978-81-8477-937-0

Chennai has many beautiful temples known for their architecture and gopurams. Chennai's famous Snake Park is located inside Guindy National Park. It is popular with both locals and tourists.

Factastic

The Tamil film industry, known as Kollywood, the second-largest film industry in India after Bollywood, is based in the city.

Tamil and English are the two languages that are widely spoken in Chennai. The local dishes are *sambar*, *rasam*, *upma*, *vada*, *idli* and *dosa*.

Chennai is the cultural capital of India. It is known for its classical dance shows and Hindu temples.

The people of Chennai are fond of music and dance. Every year, a music festival is organised where performances of traditional Carnatic music artists are featured. Chennai is also known for Bharatnatyam, a classical dance form that originated in Tamil Nadu.

I Care...

In Chennai, Carnatic music and classical music programmes are organised annually. Children are encouraged to learn these arts early. We ought to be proud of our culture and art and try to preserve them.

Explore

Find out the names of some popular Carnatic music singers and Bharatnatyam dancers.

The Governor of Tamil Nadu, the Chief Minister of the state and other ministers and government officials live in the city.

Factastic

Chennai city is governed by the Corporation of Chennai. Established in 1688, it is the oldest corporation in India.

gopurams: a tower at the entrance of a temple

 ISBN 978-81-8477-937-0

Quiz Time

1. Fill in the blanks to complete the paragraph.

__________ is the capital of the Indian state of Tamil Nadu. It was formerly known as __________. It is the __________ largest metropolitan city in India. Located on the __________ __________ of the Bay of Bengal, Chennai attracted traders and __________. The Portuguese traders came in the __________ century, followed by the Dutch and the British. It was during their rule that the British built __________, in 1640.

2. Indicate whether the following statements are true (T) or false (F).

a. The people of Chennai speak only Hindi. ☐

b. Guindy National Park is an important park in Chennai. ☐

c. The Santhome Basilica is a popular tourist attraction. ☐

d. *Sambar* is a local dish of Chennai. ☐

e. Chennai is located on the Indian Ocean. ☐

 ISBN 978-81-8477-937-0

3. Draw lines to match the following.

a. Film industry •		• Temple entrance
b. Gopuram •		• Classical dance
c. Bharatnatyam •		• Beach
d. Marina •		• Kollywood

4. Answer the questions.

a. Name the important industries in Chennai.

b. Name four tourist attractions in Chennai.

c. Name a famous dance form of Chennai.

d. How long is the Marina Beach?

5. Make a project on any metro city of India. Find out details about the city's history, its climate, the important industries, its major landmarks and its culture and cuisine.

You can make your project in the form of a booklet, a chart or a computer display.

ISBN 978-81-8477-937-0

How to Use an Atlas

A collection of maps compiled into an easy-to-use format is called an atlas. An atlas is a widely used resource in any classroom. Maps help us to identify and locate places around the world, learn more about the settings of stories, understand the historical and newsworthy locations and even do distance calculations. Atlases may be general and cover the entire globe, or they may be specific to geographical locations, topics or time periods. An atlas can have maps detailing the physical and political features, tourist spots, climate, natural resources, land, sea and air routes.

All maps are reduced to fit the size of the page, according to a scale. The two main types of maps according to scale are:

Large scale maps, which show great details of a small area. For example, the map of a city.

Small scale maps, which provide general information of a large area. For example, the map of a country.

NORTH is depicted at the top of all maps. Most maps have a grid of lines, which helps to locate the place. Parallels are lines that represent distances north and south of the Equator. Meridians are lines representing east and west of the Prime Meridian.

An atlas usually has an index at the end of the book. The index is an alphabetical listing of place names and their pronunciations. It gives you longitude and latitude coordinates as well.

Suppose you have to locate INDORE. Look up place name in the index. It may be given as INDORE 13 D4. Go to page 13 and locate INDORE in the grid box D4.

For teachers

A. Display a large map in your classroom. Every morning when students come, write the 'Find Out' or a 'Question of the Day' related to the map.

Questions may include:

How many states border Maharashtra?

Through which states does the Ganga River flow?

In which part of the world is Kenya?

B. Ask the students to create a map of their neighbourhood or colony. Encourage them to use their own keys or symbols. It will be interesting to see what each student chooses as an icon for the legend.

Tips

- Use atlases that are up to date. States and countries sometimes change names and borders. For example, what was once Czechoslovakia (one country) is now Czech Republic and Slovakia (two countries). Similarly, if you are using a road atlas for directions, make sure it is a recent one.
- Study the key or symbol guide to the maps. Each atlas uses different symbols. Symbols are important to know what you are looking for on the maps.
- Use the table of contents to find maps for your research.

 ISBN 978-81-8477-937-0

How to Use an Encyclopedia

An encyclopedia is a useful resource found in all libraries. An encyclopedia may be a single volume, subject specific, or multi-volume covering a wide range of topics. Because encyclopedias are so easy to use and so accessible, many people use encyclopedias as their first option for a reference tool.

Most general encyclopedias are multivolume sets and are set up in alphabetical format. Some encyclopedias may need you to know the key word or subject heading in order to find specific information covered over a variety of volumes. Some encyclopedias devote separate volumes to different subjects.

Locate the index. The index is usually in the last series of volumes and is in alphabetical order. It gives you page numbers and volume numbers to locate the article you are researching.

Read the article and pick out relevant information for your project.

For teachers

A. Pass a volume of an encyclopedia to a group of students. Ask them to go through the layout, the way the information is organised and the quickest way to locate an entry. Challenge each group to compile an encyclopedia on any topic. Topics could be children's authors, unique inventions, historical sites in Asia, etc.

B. Ask the students to read an entry on any animal of their choice. Encourage the students to write a newspaper article or a poem using all the details and facts from the entry.

Tips

- Look out for other cross-references that can broaden your topic and provide new insight into your research.
- Pay attention to the maps, graphs and pictures in the article.
- The outline, provided for longer articles, is a helpful reference tool when organising your writing.
- Refer to authors correctly. The information on authors is either in the introductory material or in the index.

B

B

*BAHAMAS ➾ *CARIBBEAN SEA & ISLANDS
*BAHRAIN ➾ *MIDDLE EAST

*BALKANS
The Balkan Peninsula extends into the western end of the Mediterranean Sea. The region has a long history of political and religious division.

KEY FACTS
AREA 200,000 sq. mi. (518,000 sq. km)
POPULATION 50,000,000
COUNTRIES 9
LARGEST COUNTRY Romania
SMALLEST COUNTRY Slovenia
RELIGIONS Islam, Orthodox, Roman Catholicism
LANGUAGES Albanian, Bosnian, Bulgarian, Croatian, Macedonian, Romanian, Serbian, Slovenian, Turkish

The Balkan states include the countries of Albania, Bulgaria, Greece, and Romania, plus the countries that once made up Yugoslavia: Croatia, Macedonia, Bosnia and Herzegovina, Slovenia, and the new confederation (partnership) of Serbia and Montenegro.

Land and climate
This is a mountainous region: Down the coast of Croatia, Yugoslavia, and Albania strings of mountains, an extension of the European Alps, form an impressive barrier that drops down to the shore of the Adriatic Sea.

Look in the Index for: *BACH, JOHANN SEBASTIAN *BALBOA, VASCO NÚÑEZ DE

50

 ISBN 978-81-8477-937-0

How to Use the Internet

One of the most recent and popular resources for research is the Internet. The Internet is a repository of information collected from various sources. Navigating through sites and links can give you updated information. Though the Internet is a wealth of information, before proceeding on any topic, take an adult's help to determine which sites might be reliable and which might not.

For teachers

Divide the class into four groups. Give three groups a topic to research. Each of these groups will have to research from different sources. The fourth group will then review the depth and breadth of the information collected by each, and survey and compare all the sources. It can base its report on:

Which source gave the maximum amount of information?

Which source gave the better information?

Tips

- It is a good idea to sit with an adult and bookmark the sites that you will need for research. This way you can directly go to the pages you want to view.
- Before beginning the topic, write down some keywords on which you will base your research.
- Use quality, child-friendly search engines, such as Ask Jeeves Kids (www.ajkids.com) and Yahooligans! (www.yahooligans.com). You can keep a list of helpful sites near the computer for easy access.
- Quotation marks are important while conducting a topic search. If you enter your topic or key words without quotation marks around it, the search will give information about anything linked to the words. If you put the search topic in quotation marks, you will get information related to the exact words placed within quotation marks.
- If you can't read through the entire article, you can use the FIND option to locate a particular word in the article.

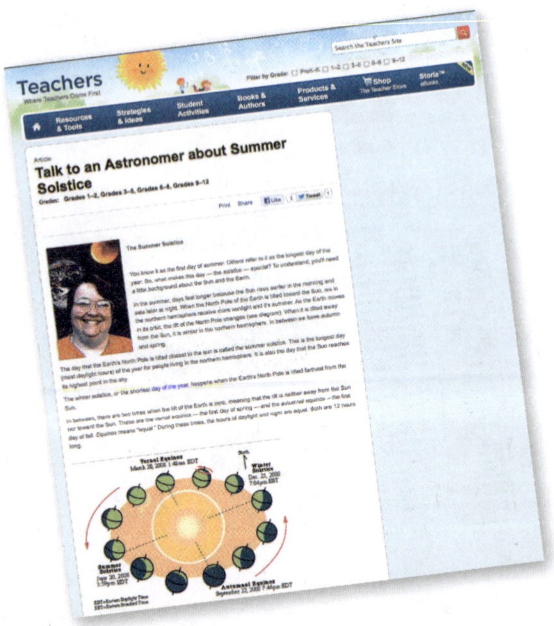

 ISBN 978-81-8477-937-0